EMPIRICAL PHILOSOPHIES
OF RELIGION

EMPIRICAL PHILOSOPHIES OF RELIGION

With Special Reference to

BOODIN · BRIGHTMAN · HOCKING
MACINTOSH and WIEMAN

By JAMES ALFRED MARTIN, JR.

Essay Index Reprint Series

BOOKS FOR LIBRARIES PRESS
FREEPORT, NEW YORK

STANDARD BOOK NUMBER:
8369-1618-2

LIBRARY OF CONGRESS CATALOG CARD NUMBER:
78-111850

PRINTED IN THE UNITED STATES OF AMERICA

PREFACE

We do not need to be reminded again that ours is a fact-minded age. That observation has been made and acted upon by many people of many interests in many fields ranging from the wondrous realms of advertising copy-writing to the more pedantic departments of academic research. From all quarters we have heard the call to be "realistic," to base all upon solid foundations of tested fact and familiar experience. The reasons for this emphasis are also well-known by now. The successful development and employment of scientific method in various areas of thought and practice have bred an enthusiasm for precision in technique which has been in many instances stimulating and in others pathetically misguided. Stresses and strains in social and economic life, accompanied by a breakdown of religious and cultural patterns which had been accepted for years, have forced men into a frantic search for the stable and enduring in practical experience. These and other factors have entered into the formation of our fact-conscious culture, and the present global calamity has but given further impetus to the trend.

In America, where enthusiastic devotion to scientific technique has produced the most spectacular results in industry and other fields, the popular demand for the factual, the practical, and the workable has been especially insistent and widespread. American philosophers and theologians have registered the trend in their own distinctive fashions. Some have turned to philosophy of science in its various ramifications, some have carried the emphasis into ethics, metaphysics, and educational philosophy, and others have turned to other fields of philosophical and religious interest. As a result we have been presented with a variety of "realistic" and "empirical" systems and studies in all fields.

In this essay I have turned my attention to a few representative thinkers in contemporary liberal Protestantism who reflect the general trend described above in their treatment of certain problems in the philosophy of religion. It is evident to any one familiar with the field that the men whom I have selected for special study may hardly be said to constitute a "school." Among them there are some fundamental disagreements concerning basic issues, and each has made a distinctive contribution to recent philosophical and religious thought. But each has been motivated by the announced purpose to develop a religious philosophy which is compatible with the growing body of scientific knowledge, which makes appropriate use of scientific method in its own sphere, and which is realistic in its treatment of the more stubborn problems of religious faith and practice.

It will become apparent to the reader at the outset that the problem of definition is of central importance in a study of this type. Indeed, it is my hope that this exposition of five religious philosophies which claim to be in some sense "empirical" may serve to emphasize the need for more careful attention to this basic problem. My efforts here are primarily critical and expository, and I have contributed little towards the urgent task of positive construction. I have indicated in the final chapter some of the directions in which my own thought is moving, and I have referred to others who, in my opinion, are making significant contributions towards the solution of some of the problems raised. It is my hope that this essay may serve to bring certain fundamental issues associated with the type of religious philosophy examined here into sharper focus, and that it may clarify to some extent certain misunderstandings which have attended recent discussion of the subject.

For helpful and patient guidance in this study I am deeply grateful to Professors H. W. Schneider and J. H. Randall, Jr., of the Department of Philosophy in Columbia University, and to Professors H. P. Van Dusen and David E. Roberts of Union Theological Seminary. I am further indebted to the National Council on Religion in Higher Education for providing material assistance in research and publication as well as intellectual stimulation and encouragement through association with its Fellows. . . . I wish to acknowledge the courtesy of the following publishers and authors who have granted permission for the use of selections from the listed books:

Abingdon-Cokesbury Press—E. S. Brightman, *Religious Values; The Problem of God; The Finding of God; Moral Laws; Personality and Religion; The Future of Christianity; The Spiritual Life;* H. N. Wieman, *The Issues of Life.*

Association Press—E. S. Brightman, *Is God A Person?*

Charles Scribner's Sons—W. E. Hocking, *Types of Philosophy;* D. C. Macintosh, *The Reasonableness of Christianity; Social Religion; Personal Religion.*

Harper & Brothers—W. E. Hocking, *Thoughts On Life and Death; What Man Can Make of Man;* D. C. Macintosh, *The Problem of Religious Knowledge.*

Harvard University Press—P. A. Bertocci, *The Empirical Argument for God in Late British Thought.*

Henry Holt and Company—E. S. Brightman, *An Introduction to Philosophy; A Philosophy of Ideals.*

Longmans, Green & Company—William James, *A Pluralistic Universe.*

Prentice-Hall—E. S. Brightman, *A Philosophy of Religion.*

The Macmillan Company—J. E. Boodin, *A Realistic Universe; God and Creation*, Vols. I and II; G. P. Adams and W. P. Montague, editors, *Contemporary American Philosophy;* D. C. Macintosh, *Theology As An Empirical Science;* W. E. Hocking, *Living Religions and A World Faith;* H. N. Wieman, *Religious Experience and Scientific Method.*

Willett, Clark and Company—D. C. Macintosh and others, *Is There A God?;* H. N. Wieman, *The Growth of Religion.*

Yale University Press—W. E. Hocking, *The Meaning of God in Human Experience; Human Nature and Its Remaking; The Self, Its Body and Freedom; The Lasting Elements of Individualism.*

J. E. Boodin, *Truth and Reality; Religion of Tomorrow.*

V. Ferm, editor, *Contemporary American Theology.*

D. C. Macintosh, *The Problem of Knowledge.*

John Moore, *Theories of Religious Experience.*

H. N. Wieman, *The Wrestle of Religion with Truth.*

Also I am indebted to the following periodicals: *Christendom; Journal of Philosophy; Journal of Religion* (The University of Chicago Press); *Mind;* The Christian Century Press; *The Philosophical Review; The Review of Religion.*

I wish also to acknowledge the invaluable assistance of my wife, Ann Bradsher Martin, who attended to the many details of editing and publishing and who helped in many other ways with the writing of this essay.

JAMES ALFRED MARTIN, JR.

Chaplain, United States Naval Reserve

CONTENTS

1
INTRODUCTION

"L ET empiricism become associated with religion, as hitherto, through some strange misunderstanding, it has been associated with irreligion, and I believe that a new era of religion as well as of philosophy will be ready to begin".[1] It was in 1909 that William James made this prediction, and since that time many of the most influential philosophers of religion in America have devoted their best efforts to carrying out the suggested program. James himself, of course, made an original and permanent contribution to the enterprise, and his influence is evident in the writings of his successors. And, though there has been considerable disagreement among those who have sought to carry on the task begun by James as to just what "empiricism" is and what sort of "association" of empiricism with religion is most fruitful, it may be said that the various attempts to develop an empirical religious philosophy constitute a dominant and significant trend in American religious thought of the recent past.

Now some of the disagreement, if not confusion, surrounding the current use of the term "empiricism"—a confusion which at times seems to make it, no less than "experience", a "weasel-word"—may perhaps be traced to the history of empiricism itself. Dewey has pointed out in an illuminating essay that there are at least three major types of empiricism in the history of Western philosophy. Greek empiricism was based upon a conception of experience as embracing simply the accumulated information of the past, individual and social, as this was transmitted through language and through apprenticeship in the arts and crafts. Empirical knowledge, therefore, was conceived to be merely the funded information of custom and common-sense wisdom; it was what Plato called "opinion", and was contrasted with "science", which was conceived in terms of the rationalized, systematic, thought-through type of knowledge whose normative pattern was mathematics. This rationalistic ideal, in turn, was central throughout most of the ancient and medieval periods.

Then, in the eighteenth and nineteenth centuries, the dictums of rationalism and dogma seemed to become stale and too narrow for the expanding interests of men. There came then a new appeal to "experience" as something fresh and personal, tentative and exploratory, affording a new first-hand contact with nature, chiefly on the basis of sense-perception. The ideal of knowledge as a fixed system was abandoned by many, though mathematics and morals retained, for some of the early modern empiricists, a fixed status in their own spheres. Finally Hume brought to a head the individualistic and observational emphases of the new movement by reducing all relations to associations, and Bentham and Mill set about the development of a utilitarian ethic.

Recent empiricism, while retaining the notion that scientific knowledge must begin and end with public experience, has not conceived of such experience narrowly in terms of mere sensation and association. Affective, volitional, and valuational elements are seen to be parts of the whole. And the significance of experimentation, or experimentalism, as the most fruitful method for the exploration and organization of experience has been emphasized. Such method involves carefully regulated activity guided by consciously defined goals. The free and imaginative quality of hypotheses is stressed, and verification is seen to be more a matter of consequences than of origins or of "correspondence with reality".[2]

But not all recent writers who have classified themselves as empiricists stress just those emphases mentioned in the preceding paragraph. Often, as Professor Loewenberg has pointed out, the term "empirical" refers broadly to the general temperament or attitude of a thinker, to what James called the quality of "tough-mindedness".

> To describe a temper as empirical is to express in summary fashion the fundamental bias by which it is dominated, the bias for stubborn facts, immediate values, shifting forms, flexible standards, cautious opinions, disillusioned aspirations.[3]

Such a use of the term is obviously as vague and ambiguous as is the frequent use of the term "realistic" to mean essentially the same thing.

Again, "empiricism" may refer broadly to an "appeal to experience" for the foundational data used in philosophical constructions. And here again ambiguity arises with the question as to what constitutes "experience" and as to which types of experience are to be taken as normative. Is there some one kind of experience in terms of which other kinds are to be interpreted, such as the "immediate experience" of Bergson or the kind of mystical experience which led Royce and, as we shall see, Hocking, to call the mysti the thoroughgoing empiricist? Or is normative experience more properly conceived in terms of sensation, as the early modern empiricists held, or perhaps more precisely in terms of particular, changing, and contingent "sense data", as the modern positivists hold? Is "experience" to have a primarily subjective connotation and refer to "contents of conscious awareness" as held, we shall see, by certain idealists; or is it to mean primarily that abstract and quantitative "experience" of the natural world emphasized in certain sciences, in which the subjective element is reduced to the minimum? Or, finally, may the term "experience" refer, more liberally and perhaps more fruitfully, to all aspects of that "enjoyment and suffering" which constitutes man's intercourse with nature, including objective and subjective, quantitative and qualitative, remote and immediate, abstract and gross features: the public world of daily living? We shall maintain that this latter conception of "experience", as constituting the "given" with which a thoroughgoing empiricism must begin and end, is most appropriate and least ambiguous.

But the term "empirical" is also used in contemporary discussion to designate a *method* for getting at, organizing, and interpreting the data of experience. And here again there is ambiguity. Some thinkers mean by "empirical method" simply "all the ways of the mind involved in inquiry", including intuition and critical investigation, deduction and induction, a-priori and a-posteriori factors, the emphases traditionally associated with rationalism as well as those more precisely designated as "empirical" by other thinkers. Our present study will include illustrations of this use of "empirical method", and we may say at this point that we agree with Loewenberg when he writes that this usage "exhibits in its nakedness the fallacy of the suppressed correlative",[4] which is to say that it makes any alternative method meaningless and is thus a useless, if not confusing, addition to philosophical terminology. There is no profit in speaking of empirical method unless it be clearly understood that there are other methods with clearly defined emphases of their own which are by definition *not* empirical.

But some philosophers have used the term with less ambiguity. They have meant by it a method of inquiry which is broadly instrumental, operational, or experimental; which is open and cautious in its approach and tentative in its conclusions; a method which, in other words, is patterned after those working procedures which have been so fruitful in the inquiries of the natural sciences. Such a method is limited in its operations to the realm of the publicly observable and the recurrent, the communicable and the controllable. Its goal is the more precise delineation of these aspects of experience for the sake of more accurate predictions concerning the course of future happenings, in order to make possible a more intelligent control of experience in the interest of clearly defined aims. When empirical method is conceived in this manner, the question of definite alternatives is left open, such alternatives including methods which could be broadly designated as discursive, dialectical, or rationalistic. We shall maintain in this study that this latter conception of empirical method is more clearly in line with the historical development of empiricism itself; that it may be employed with least ambiguity and confusion in contemporary discussion, technical and otherwise; and that, in conjunction with the liberal understanding of "experience" suggested above, it lends itself most satisfactorily to a precisely defined empirical philosophy.[5]

The term "empirical philosophy of religion" has been used with all three of the connotations suggested above. Sometimes it refers simply to the "empirical" or "realistic" attitude of the thinker, suggesting that he is attempting to take seriously all of the facts, no matter how "stubborn", which should be taken account of in a religious philosophy. Again it refers to the attempt on the part of the philosopher to base his thought upon an appeal to "experience". This, in turn, may mean an appeal to various areas of experience and a defense of a theistic "hypothesis" of some sort as the best "explanation" of experience; or it may mean an appeal to some type of specifically religious experience as affording the normative data for a philosophy of religion. Or, again, it may mean that the philosopher seeks to employ some form of empirical method in the interpretation of such data as seem significant for his purposes. We may say that all of the thinkers who figure in our present study exhibit something of the empirical temper and attitude as broadly defined above. But we shall see that they differ considerably with respect to what types of experience are of significance for their purposes, as well as in their basic understandings of the word "experience" itself. And we shall also discover a considerable divergence in their understanding of what constitutes the empirical method in terms of which such experience is to be interpreted.

The question of just where the historical roots of modern empirical religious philosophy are to be found is complex, and it is perhaps not appropriate to go into the question in any detail here. In the Christian tradition, of course, a kind of "theocentric rationalism" dominated most apologetic thinking until near the end of the medieval period. This type of apologetic was in keeping with the general Platonic character of thought in the Middle Ages; but, with the emergence of the scientific spirit, rationalistic theology was challenged, and the Thomistic synthesis, embodying Thomas' five quasi-empirical "proofs" of the existence of God, marked a turning point in the development of "natural theology." It was, however, only in the modern period, after Kant's critical attack upon all forms of rationalistic theology, that the earliest attempts at what is now called empirical religious philosophy were made. These attempts embodied, in general, appeals to the "practical reason" and to the "religious consciousness" as affording a firm foundation for faith.

The appeal to religious experience as affording a more trustworthy foundation for belief than assent to or demonstration of theological propositions has, of course, been a perennial feature of religious history. John M. Moore, in his study of this problem,[6] has pointed out that intellectual and cult-centered eras in religious thought are usually followed by periods of revival, in which inward piety and the "fruits of the spirit" are stressed, and in which experience takes precedence over theoretical belief. One recurrent motive for this is the attempt to simplify dogma, but there is also an apologetic aim at justifying beliefs on the ground of their experimental basis. Moore suggests that the modern emphasis upon religious experience is also in harmony with the general individualism of the modern mind, involving the appeal of liberal culture to individual personality and experience as basic to the development and defense of intellectual and institutional structures. It has also accompanied the development of empirical philosophy as such.

The first outstanding religious philosopher in the Christian tradition to apply in detail the method of appealing to the "religious consciousness" for the normative data in this field was, of course, Schleiermacher. It is true that he did not call his philosophy of religion "empirical", perhaps because of the narrower connotation which the term bore in his day. But his "descriptive" and "historical" method and his emphasis upon the "religious consciousness" as over against rationalism, Protestant scholasticism, and ethical theism are features of many subsequent developments in the school. Similarly, Albrecht Ritschl's emphasis upon the historical and the appeal to religious value-judgments suggests many of the emphases incorporated in later developments of empirical religious philosophy— though his rejection of metaphysics has not been shared by those who are in other respects his successors. It may be said that it is to these two men, Schleiermacher and Ritschl, with their respective and sometimes conflicting emphases, that modern empirical philosophers of religion are chiefly indebted.

The appeal to the "religious consciousness" has taken many forms, and we shall see it employed in various ways by the subjects of the present study. It has involved appeals to "feeling" of various types, to "the experience of believing", "the experience of the holy", the "feeling of meanings", and to various forms of "intuition" and mystical insight. Again, there has been a more general appeal to "life-experience as a whole", or to religious experience "taken as any experience in relation to the whole of experience". Indeed, some of those who have made analytical studies of some of the various ways in which "religious experience" has been used in recent religious thought have concluded that the term itself has now become so ambiguous as to be practically devoid of definite meaning.[7]

Similarly, the appeal to value-experience has appeared in various ways. P. A. Bertocci, in his study of "the empirical argument for God" in recent

British thought, shows that the appeal to value and to forms of the "moral argument" has played an important role in the thought of writers like Martineau, Pringle-Pattison, and Sorley, who are classified by him as empirical theologians. He is, of course, using the term broadly, to include those theologians who hold that "argument for God must be based upon the known facts of experience", including value-experience, and "who deny the validity of a priori arguments for theism and profess to proceed inductively to the conclusion that the existence of a certain kind of God is the best explanation of the whole of man's experience".[8] Whether this be a fruitful use of the term "empirical" in this connection we shall discuss further in our study, when we consider similar views as held by certain American thinkers. We merely wish to point out here that all of the British thinkers treated by Bertocci emphasize the significance of value-experience in the development of "inductive" theology. Those who, like F. R. Tennant, stress chiefly the overall theological character of the world as interpreted by modern science, include a form of the "moral argument" within the teleological.

Among the Americans whom we shall study we shall find the appeal to value-experience playing various roles. In the thought of idealists, such as Hocking and Brightman, ethical analysis becomes the basis for a more or less rationalistic deduction of the necessity for a supreme ideal being. Macintosh, on the other hand, while insisting upon a distinction between "normative" or "valuational" and "empirical" theology, includes an "intuition" of certain values as an integral feature of religious perception. And Wieman, by adopting a naturalistic view of values, maintains that God as supreme value is a perceptible natural process. But the American thinkers differ from the British, chiefly, it would seem, in the stress which some of them put upon the significance of religious experience as such, and in the attempt on the part of some to employ a quasi-scientific empirical method in interpreting distinctively religious data.

Now the chief rivals of empirical philosophy, both general and religious, in American thought, have been transcendental idealism and rationalistic realism, though these latter have also embodied, at least in certain systems, some features of empiricism. Perhaps the most picturesque and influential expression of this rivalry is to be found in the contrast between James and Royce. It is expressed both in their influence upon and differences with each and in their influences upon the development of the thought of the men whom we shall study. And the struggle is not simply *between* James and Royce; it is also reflected in the intellectual development of these men themselves. There was a considerable shift of emphasis on the part of Royce from the a priori and ontological arguments employed in *The Religious Aspect of Philosophy* (1885) to his attempt to deal with "the human and

empirical aspects of some of the leading and essential ideas of Christianity" in *The Problem of Christianity* (1913). And President Bixler has
shown in his book on James' philosophy of religion that the conflict between the "tender-minded" appeal of the Absolute and the "tough-minded"
challenge of melioristic empiricism was resolved by James only after considerable struggle—if, indeed, it was ever fully resolved.[9]

But the story of empirical religious philosophy in American thought of
the recent past is not a mere continuation of the debate between James and
Royce; rather it presents various revisions of both Jamesian empiricism
and Royceian idealism in original and suggestive systems, revisions which
take account of significant developments in the general field of philosophy
since their time and which were made possible, in part, by the fruitfulness
of their debate. Among the figures whom we shall study both Hocking and
Boodin acknowledge the direct and important influence of both James and
Royce upon their thought. Brightman was led to contrast James not only
with Royce but also with the personalistic idealism of B. P. Browne. Macintosh abandoned an early Hegelian position as a result of the influence of
the Chicago School of pragmatists. And Wieman has been influenced by
Royce through Hocking, while he has subjected idealism to criticisms suggested by Dewey and Whitehead.

Thus we shall see, as our study progresses, how idealism has sought to be
empirical, and how such empiricism differs from other forms. For it is one
purpose of our study to show, through a summary exposition of certain
important types, some of the divergent patterns which recent empirical
religious philosophies have followed. It may be that such an exposition will
serve to clarify, to some degree, the ambiguity and confusion which seem
to surround the subject in contemporary discussion. In this exposition we
shall attempt to discover whether there are certain emphases shared by all
of those interested in the development of such a philosophy, and also to
delineate some of the chief points of misunderstanding and disagreement
among them. As a result we may be able, in conclusion, to suggest an approach to religious philosophy which could be called "empirical" with a
minimum of misunderstanding on the part of philosophers and laymen
alike.

At the same time we may raise certain questions concerning the religious
assumptions and the theological consequences involved in these attempts
to develop an empirical religious philosophy. The thinkers selected for
study all stand within the Christian tradition. To what extent and in what
sense do they claim to have specifically Christian positions and to what extent is empirical religious philosophy assumed to be "objective" and "universal" in the same sense that science is? Are any significant modifications
or limitations with reference to basic theological concepts involved in the

attempt to be empirical in this realm? And if, as C. C. J. Webb has put it, "the character of combined ultimacy and intimacy is the hall-mark of religion", to what extent and in what manner may religious experience and conviction be accounted for or judged in terms of an empirical method which is in some definite sense scientific? These are some of the questions which we may bear in mind as we examine certain features of five empirical philosophies of religion which have been of considerable influence in recent American religious thought.

EMPIRICAL IDEALISM

I: W. E. Hocking, *Objective Idealist*

THE philosophy of William Ernest Hocking (b. 1873) illustrates rather clearly the competing influences of absolute idealism and experimental empiricism in recent American thought. Though we have followed the procedure of others in classifying him as an objective idealist, those familiar with his writings are aware that his richly stimulating and in many respects original system does not lend itself easily to simple classification. Indeed, he himself has professed difficulty in labelling his position, referring to it as "realism . . . mysticism . . . idealism also, its identity not broken";[1] as "a realism of social experience, or . . . social realism, or more truly a realism of the Absolute, not far removed from Absolute idealism";[2] and as including a "transfigured naturalism".[3] We shall see that there is some basis for each of these designations, but it is not our primary purpose to determine just which of them best describes his thought as a whole. What is more significant for our purposes is the fact that the idealism of Royce and the pragmatism of James seem to be the most clearly distinguishable influences in the formation of his philosophy, though he has significantly modified the contributions of each in his own suggestive construction, along with the additional fact that one of his chief interests, and the field of some of his most significant work, has been the philosophy of religion. He thus seems to be a particularly appropriate figure for our study.

A brief glance at certain features of Hocking's intellectual and religious development before proceeding to an exposition of his thought may be of some value. He has written that the religious environment of his early life was "concrete, vivid, and regulatory"; in his home "Bunyan and Milton were understood to be fanciful enough, but not wholly false to the situation". His early intellectual and religious interests were characterized by a wide-ranging curiosity about a number of subjects and included some "semi-mystical" religious experiences, connected in part with periods of convalescence from illness. Such experiences, he says, were considered by him to be significant affairs, in which "there was no emancipation from any ill of fortune, but a new immunity from overthrow in any of them."[4] His introduction to philosophy was through the writings of some of the nineteenth century naturalists, who stimulated a growing interest on his part in science. Finding an attraction in mathematics, he prepared himself for a career as a civil engineer. But certain personal crises, coupled with questions raised by more modern accounts of physics, caused him to turn from Herbert Spencer, whose disciple he had become, to seek a new intellectual orientation. At this period he began to read James, and he was so greatly impressed that he decided to study at Harvard.

When he arrived in Cambridge, however, he found that James would be absent for two years. So he studied ethics and history of philosophy with G. H. Palmer, was introduced to idealism by Dickinson Miller, and began a study of German thought under the guidance of Münsterberg. Though Santayana was there, Hocking was not attracted by him. But he found Royce to be "a man of intellectual majesty and moral greatness" and was partially won over to Royce's philosophy. When James returned, however, Hocking found him to be something of the "liberator" whom he had expected. Nevertheless, he found himself unable to subscribe to all of James' doctrines. Thus he began to develop, from his early mysticism and supplanted naturalism, an original viewpoint stimulated by both James and Royce but identical with the views of neither. He later went to Germany for further study, where he came under the influence of Natorp, Husserl, Paulsen, Dilthey, Windelband, and Rickert, and where he began a careful and prolonged study of Kant, Fichte, and Hegel. Upon returning to America he set about the concrete development of his own system. During most of his academic career he has been at Yale and Harvard.

In his earliest and most extensive study in the philosophy of religion, Hocking indicated his empirical bent in the statement that "God must be known in experience if at all".[5] The popularity of "antirationalistic" interpretations of religion, which would root faith in intuition, instinct, or feeling, clearly indicated, he felt, a "disaffection from the religion of reason, and from its philosophical framework, absolute idealism".[6] Such disaffection he felt to be valid, in that absolute idealism in religion is "unfinished"; it cannot do justice to variety, change, growth, personality, and freedom, and it "does not give sufficient credence to the authoritative Object . . . shows no adequate comprehension of the attitude of *worship*";[7] the particular and the historical are left out. Thus he would address himself to a fresh study of religion as it appears in human experience, attempting to take account of affective and volitional as well as rational elements.

Feeling, "the total response to the total situation", cannot be left out of account in cognition, he says. James' insistence that there must be a "cutting behind" dead and unwieldy ideas, and Bergson's insistence upon a peculiar and unanalysable type of cognition of self, time and continuity are justified. However, Hocking holds that it must not be forgotten that feeling is always moving towards cognition; objectification and knowledge are always the goal. The "working" of an idea in experience becomes fruitful only in so far as the guiding rational concept is clarified thereby. Thus, while the Bergsonian and pragmatic criticisms are justified, the rationalistic ideal remains relevant.[8]

A chief contribution of intuition is knowledge of wholes, and of The Whole. Such intuition is always "running ahead" of intellect, in so far as the store of objects for analytic intellection seems to be inexhaustible. Yet intuition must always be accompanied by and expressed in conceptual thought.[9] The idea of the Whole, however, is really basic in knowledge, which proceeds, not from part-to-whole, but like a germ-cell, in the direction of a more complex differentiation while retaining something of an original unity. That which develops in knowledge is understanding of "the internal complexity and detail, middle-world of experience". The Whole is not only knowable, but is "the one thing permanently known".[10] Yet the idea of the Whole is not purely subjective or a priori; if one had not *experienced* the Whole he could never have an idea of it. Neither the experience of the Whole nor that of parts is reducible to the other.

And, by the same token, the idea of the Whole cannot be accounted for simply on the basis of pure feeling, even though our deepest and most primitive awareness of it must be described in terms of "intuition", an intuition whose content is not immediately given but is forever in the making. Though we may give no final predicate to the Whole, we should not infer that it is nothing; nor does the addition of new predicates necessarily mean that the old ones were false. Nevertheless, throughout all activity the Whole-idea as such remains stable (and forms, as we shall see, the basis for Hocking's methodology, the "empirical dialectic"). Its presence is intense and total; therefore we must conclude, thinks Hocking, that only objectivity can "stir the soul" with such total effect. "Deeper than idea is Idea", he writes; the idea-world is the world of real objects, not subjective feelings.[11] Thus there is at least one "meaning of God in human experience" which is grasped intuitively but has the force of normative objectivity, in that our developing knowledge of part-particulars which is commonly called "objective knowledge" presupposes it for its own meaning. For "it is the mark of religious passion that a specific *view of the whole* makes conscious connection with one's practical ultimata".[12]

This general knowledge of God as the Whole is seen to be empirically concrete as it is related more definitely to natural and social experience. Historically, religious experiences have been associated with powerful natural objects and social crises, and the two are actually inseparable: nature becomes religiously charged when it is personalized and animated, and social forces are regarded as of religious value only in a cosmic setting. But the sense of awe and fear which characterizes such experiences must rest, Hocking believes, upon a previous conception of the Whole, which is the basis of all valuations and makes possible the sense of mystery in the *"mysterium tremendum et fascinans"*, and which may be interpreted as "the World judging man". The "knowledge of ignorance" which is at the root of all speculative activity presupposes a sense of mystery, which means, "I know not, but it is known". "It seems to me, then, that the original source of knowledge of God is an experience which might be described as an experience of *not being alone in knowing the world,* and especially the world of Nature".[13] It is this religious confidence which makes the employment of scientific method itself possible and affords justification and stimulus for moral and social effort. Faith and patience in such effort are possible because of a religious "taste of infinite attainment".

"At the source of all religion", then, "we find an experience of God as an Other Knower of our world, already in close relation to self, and also in some natural bond with our social and physical experience".[14] But "Other Knower" means "Other Mind", which affords an explanation of our social knowledge of nature and our personal knowledge of other minds. Our knowledge of nature is of nature as social, that is, as a common matrix in which each knower is "in" the other's experience. Yet social experience itself, according to Hocking, can be accounted for only in terms of an Other Mind, other than any individual mind or any group of minds, because our "natural" knowledge of others is always only of other bodies, the natural "metaphors" of minds; direct social experience is impossible. Most alternative theories of our knowledge of other minds really presuppose the idea as given, when the real question is How is it given? The three constant elements in all experience are nature, self, and other mind. These cannot be explained in terms of each other, but only in terms of an Other Mind through whom social experience and thus the "objectivity" of nature are meaningful.

> If only I were independant of Nature, I might think Nature independent of Self. But since Nature *obstinate* is Nature *creative,* and creative of mind; since my deepest roots and those of all co-experiencing mind are in her deepest objectivity, I cannot clear Nature of *selfhood,* though I can well clear her of my own self or of any other particular self . . . it is thus because the empirical factors of experience extend thus through my whole selfhood that this not-self (not *my*self) is known in positive terms as Other-self.[15]

The Other is not society, present or pantemporal, since such a consensus presupposes a prior unity; communication presupposes a oneness in objectivity. Genuine social experience can therefore be known as such only if there be some "prior" social experience, something already known as common object. And, since each particular self is an empirical knower of nature, no conglomeration of such knowers could yield the "original" social experience upon which the "objectivity" of nature depends. Nor would any one all-comprehending *passive* Knower suffice; such a being would Himself be dependent and self-enclosed. Thus, Hocking concludes, "we have been led by the successive requirements of our logic to the position that our first and fundamental social experience is an experience of God. . . . It is through the knowledge of God that I am able to know men". There is, indeed, a divine compulsion to express the divine companionship in social relations. And our knowledge of God is thus as "literal" as our knowledge of nature and society.

> To be literal means to be real in the same definite and particular fashion that we surmise in sensation, and realize in the precise work of physical science. Sensation may supply, as it were, a missing dimension to our thought of God. God must be not less real than Nature, not less definitely here and new than these impressive objective facts.[16]

"Proofs" of God's existence then become simply the rational interpretation of what is found in gross experience.

The broader sources of religious knowledge, then, are to be found in natural and social experience. But the specifically religious experiences are those of powerful natural phenomena and of social crises, experiences characterized by a sense of awe and mystery which leads to a recognition of ignorance and stimulates theoretical and practical activity. And the decisive and unique "experience of The Whole" is to be discovered in religious worship and mystical experience. The worth of worship lies in its ambition to find the ultimate powerful reality to which man must adjust himself and by which he is judged. Worship seeks perspective on all the major issues of life; bringing all established habits of thought under judgment, it makes possible fresh perceptions. It is an "essay in detachment", beyond the partial detachments of art and science. In mysticism this aim at detachment is expressed in the *via negativa*; concentration and unification of thought prepares the way for the "loss" of the self in deeper insights. And the experience itself involves a realization that the process must be completed "from without", through "grace".[17]

But the "valid" mystical experience, in Hocking's judgment, is not a matter of "pure thought" alone; rather "purity of heart" is a necessary moral precondition. And, through the "principle of alternation", worship must bear fruit in work, and vice-versa. The sense of disconnection from rationality and conventionality serves to fructify both, and the deepened sense of solitude and individuality affords a true basis for genuine sociality.

In worship "the worshipper has exercised his freedom, perhaps the first and last freedom possessed by the human spirit, to consent to an empirical apparition of the real." Thus, as Royce suggested the mystic is the "thorough-going empiricist".

> But the mystic's peculiarity is that he applies this method to objects which empiricists generally insist cannot be given in any such immediate, unreasoned manner, namely to totals not elements; to resultants not to factors; and, finally, to God himself.[18]

Through this interpretation of mystical experience Hocking can claim a specific empirical grounding for his objective idealism, resting it on the certain knowledge of a crucial Object, through a specific kind of experience.

Some questions may be raised at this point concerning this type of appeal to experience in the construction of a religious philosophy; others will develop in the course of our study, particularly with reference to a similar conception of religious experience held by Professor Wieman. Macintosh has his own criticism of the appeal to this type of experience, while Brightman criticizes all appeals to specific types of religious experience as finally normative for the philosophy of religion.

Perhaps the major question to be raised is whether the "experience of the Whole" is truly *an* experience, of one "object" among others. That the "idea of the whole" is a working idea of cognition and understanding is perhaps undebatable. But, as Hocking himself insists, the "experience of the Whole" is different in kind from all other types of experience. Surely all sensory experiences, at least, are experiences of definite particulars, or perhaps of definable complexes, and thus of "parts". Even value-experiences have specific referents. But the experience of the Whole is ultimately undifferentiated. Is it, then, *an* experience of a definite *object,* with definable relations to other objects? If not, is it correct to maintain that the idea of the Whole has more than functional relevance to the rest of experience, or is more than a *co-implicate* of gross experience *when interpreted in a certain way?* It is surely an idea with definite functional meaning, but why Hocking thinks that it must be more than this is not quite clear. He is careful to indicate that the experience of the Whole is to be judged, at least partially, in terms of its fruits in action. What kind of significance it has apart from its functional efficacy and its character as a co-implicate or "regulative ideal" of all possible "partial and unfinished experience" it is hard to see. Since it is so dissimilar from all other "sufferings and undergoings" usually called "experience" the use of this term to cover the apprehension of "the Whole" may well be misleading.

But what is the character of the specific experience of the Whole as illustrated in mysticism? It may be remarked that Hocking limits himself to one type of "valid" mysticism, which is activistic, and moralistic. He criticizes those mystics who declare that God is "one, immediate, and ineffable" on the ground that they mistake a true psychological report of their experience for a metaphysical proposition; from the fact that one's *experience* has seemed "one, immediate, and ineffable" it does not follow that God himself is to be described in these terms, he says.[19] Now it is true that a psychological account of *any* kind of experience is possible, and that this account is not necessarily exhaustive in the determination of its validity. But if one makes such a judgment "psychologising" variant types of mystical experience, where are the criteria by which the truly transubjective and valid is to be determined? In other words, is the mystical "experience of the Whole" described by Hocking self-vindicating, or is it to a large extent determined by the interpretive concepts set by the author, concepts derived in part from his analysis of the problem of knowledge, in part from broadly Christian value-judgments? Is it the experience of the whole of reality, or of the whole-*ness* of the subject's own experience? Is the experience to be had universally under a definable set of conditions? Or, if the appeal is intended to be an appeal to "pure" experience, after the manner of James, with whose conception of mysticism that of Hocking, we may remark, has much in common, does it not overlook some of the intricate relations of theory to experience? As John M. Moore has pointed out,

> the fundamental ideas and valuations which the mystic has received from his cultural environment enter into and determine the character of his mystical experience. This does not mean, of course, that mystical experience is simply the product of a philosophy. Rather . . . the philosophy conditions the experience, and the experience in turn may serve to modify the philosophy.[20]

We cannot examine here the great number of types and theories of mystical experience which have been stressed in recent thought.[21] The point is that *variety* is perhaps the most evident feature of such types and theories. If one seeks an empirical grounding for a philosophical or religious concept, it is of dubious value to appeal to a selected **type of experience**, since the selection itself indicates that the validity of the experience is bound up with the validity of its interpretive concepts. This comment we shall have occasion to elaborate with reference to appeals to other types of religious experience for knowledge of the "subject-matter" of theology. It is enough here to suggest that the significance of the type of experience, if it be *an* experience, described by Hocking, is bound up with the correctness of his analysis of the problem of knowledge as such, and with his interpretation of the data involved in natural and social experience.

It is perhaps not appropriate here to offer an extended technical critique of his analysis in this respect. It may be pointed out, however, that much of the strength of his argument depends upon the thesis that knowledge of self, nature, and society must necessarily involve some sort of "concrete a-priori" ideas of these factors in the total knowledge-situation. And this involves, in turn, the basic proposition that "deeper than idea is Idea". Now it may be asked whether a proposition of this sort is possible unless one, following the lead of much traditional idealism, begins with the assumption that being somehow depends upon knowing. Hocking is well aware of the subjectivistic consequences which have followed the employment of this presupposition by other idealists, and he is intent on demonstrating the objectivity of Nature and other minds. But it seems that he is led to posit a cosmic "Other Knower" in order to accomplish this only because he cannot conceive of objectivity apart from the knowledge of some Subject. And this, it would seem, is essentially the same thesis which has led other idealists to that subjectivism which he would avoid. His "empiricism", in other words, is restricted by the assumption that certain basic categories of experience must ultimately be "idea", and that we can recognize the "concrete a-priori" character of these categories only if we have somehow "experienced" them "prior" to the part-experiences which they are supposed to make intelligible. Does this not involve an unfortunate ambiguity in the use of the term "experience"? We should maintain that the natural and social experience to which a less ambiguous empiricism would appeal for its foundational data is simply and solely the concrete, particular, public, changing and "unfinished" experience which Hocking feels called upon to "explain", "through successive stages of logic," in terms of a priori concepts more usually associated with rationalistic philosophy. A more consistent empiricism would seek rather to account for natural, social, and personal contexts of experience in terms of each other. Indeed, the empiricism of idealists like Hocking might be called a "rationalism in reverse". It shares with a more whole-hearted empiricism a respect for the gross data of public experience and seeks, as some absolute idealism has not done, to take seriously the job of "saving the appearances". But the interpretive concepts which it feels called upon to employ in this procedure are rooted, we believe, in the same "subjectivist fallacy" which generates the basic concept of "appearances" as applied to public experience as such. And when empirical status is claimed for such interpretive concepts or "concrete a-prioris", not only on the basis of their being demanded by "successive stages" of logical analysis, but also on the basis of their having somehow to be "experienced" *as a prioris,* "prior to" the part-experiences which they are said to "explain"; then "experience" is indeed being used, to borrow Professor Perry's term, as a "weasel-word".

This ambiguity is most clearly reflected in Hocking's defense of the ontological argument for the existence of God as being at the same time the only persuasive and necessary argument, and also truly "empirical". This argument, he says, is the "only one which is faithful to the history, the anthropology of religion. It is the only proof of God." He accepts the Kantian criticism of the cosmological argument, and he feels that the validity of the teleological depends upon it. Any argument which proceeds from the bare character of nature as it *is* and seeks not to "go beyond" it in establishing the case for theism really succeeds only in "refunding" the problems of experience and simply reflects the world as it is. The God-idea derived thereby is thus a useless addition to knowledge; it affords another way of saying "what is, is". The historically and philosophically authentic basis of theism, on the contrary, makes the God-idea meaningful as that upon which the knowledge and existence of the world depends, as the Whole, the Ground, the Infinite, "Other Knower", and so on. Thereby the objects of part-experience are rendered intelligible in their relation to the Whole as predicate to subject—or perhaps as quality to substance. Now of course such a conception of God raises innumerable questions concerning the independent existence of the parts and their actual relation to a Whole or Other Knower which or Who is also said to have a type of independent and "transcendent" existence; reasoning of this type has led to pantheism, "panentheism", and many positions other than theism; we cannot investigate the complex problem of alternatives here. It is significant, however, that by advocating a form of the ontological argument as the sole basis for theism Hocking dissociates himself from certain features of the kind of "inductive" empirical theology espoused by some of the British thinkers mentioned earlier and, in varying respects, by other thinkers who figure in our own study.

In any event, Hocking feels that the ontological argument is self-authenticating. The discovery of the lack of self-sufficiency of all parts of nature and of the self as dependent upon nature produces the dialectical movement to the idea of the real as Creative Spirit. And if this idea were not a "true" idea man could never have entertained it; "for my idea can set me outside of nature only as in my experience I have already broken away from the spell of the natural world. . . . This idea carries its reality with it." It is "empirical" and not a priori because (by definition?) such an idea could not have arisen apart from some appropriate "experience". "It is impossible that my idea should be a 'mere' idea, for it is only possible for me to take this standpoint, external to nature and myself, in idea in so far as I do at the same time take it in experience also. . . . The ontological argument, in its true form, is a report of experience." And the "true" form of the argument, he says is not thus: I have an idea of God, therefore God exists. But rather thus: I have an idea of God, therefore I have an experience of God. Reality can only be proved by the ontological argument; and, conversely, the ontological argument can only be applied to reality. But in so far as reality dwells in Self, or Other Mind, or Nature, an ontological argument may be stated in proof of their existence. Thus the Cartesian certitude may with greater validity be put into this form: I think myself, therefore I exist . . . I have an idea of physical Nature, Nature exists . . . In whatever sense I can think the independence of beings, in that sense independence obtains between them. That which is most independent of me, namely the Other Mind, has been the first object of our ontological findings. The object of certain knowledge has this threefold structure, Self, Nature, and Other Mind; and God, the appropriate object of ontological proof, includes these three.[22]

Here again, then, is the same ambiguity which we found in Hocking's appeal to "experience" for knowledge of God. Indeed, he says that "the ontological argument may be regarded as a logical epitome of what we there (in the analysis of natural and social knowledge) . . . came upon".[23] And once again we must ask whether it is fruitful to call the deduction of a Whole or Other Knower from the logical analysis of gross experience, a deduction which itself presupposes an original independence of self, nature, and society, on the one hand, and the assumption that being is somehow dependent upon being known, on the other, "empirical" or "literal". We maintain, rather, that the assertion of such a proposition as "I have an idea . . . *therefore* I have an experience . . ." completely reverses that approach to philosophical analysis which, in the sphere of religion or elsewhere, could with least ambiguity be termed "empirical", historically and logically. In the case of Hocking's defense of theism, then, it would seem that the idealist is "empirical" only in the sense that he does sincerely seek to take account of affective and volitional as well as rational elements in knowledge, and of the particular and "unfinished" in experience; but what he "finds" in his analysis is dependent upon assumptions and goals more precisely defined as rationalistic.

Just as he feels it necessary to supplement and qualify the account of what "experience" actually presents, as compared with the accounts of other empiricists, so Hocking feels that the philosophical method which can prove most fruitful in the interpretation of such experience must embody more than a simple experimentalism. He has often acknowledged his indebtedness to James and other pragmatists and instrumentalists for insight into the value of free, tentative, and objective inquiry, and at an early date adopted as a part of his philosophy what he called a "negative pragmatism", summarised in the statement that "that which does *not* work is not true". A theory without consequences, which makes no difference or a bad difference to men, which "lowers the capacity of men to meet the stress of existence, or diminishes the worth to them of such existence as they have . . . is somehow false", he wrote. And it was on this basis that he challenged many of the religious consequences of absolute idealism. It is true that knowledge may be tentative, that "truth must wait", while action may not, and thus a kind of "will-to-believe" is pertinent.[24] Furthermore, he has constantly insisted upon the freedom of scientific inquiry and the worth of the "liberal" spirit. But he has offered extensive criticisms of that form of pragmatism which takes simply and finally the notion that working constitutes meaning and truth[25] and has insisted at the same time that the objectivity and tentativeness of scientific inquiry itself is possible only if it be based upon a central conviction of certainty and a sense of ultimate attainment. "Though there may be unfinished truth", he says, "yet the finishing demands an *identity* which is never destroyed or misplaced in the finishing. . . . Ultimate co-operation with God in world-making we have; not, however, in God-making."[26] Meaning and working do not always correspond; objects must be more than interests; and there is and must be such a thing as "eternal truth"; these are, according to him, basic propositions which any adequate methodology must take into account. Since science aims at "stability" in its conclusions, it is really aiming at conclusions which are "true always". Decisive action presupposes belief in something fixed and certain, and men whose actions have been of most significance in history have been men who so believed. In other words, though it has been the genius and glory of the modern scientific spirit to realize that man's body of knowledge and belief is not static, nevertheless it must also be insisted that "change does not eat out what is true in it." The working sciences must employ certain "a-prioris" which can be "tested" only by presupposing them. And science is necessarily committed to at least one *ethical* "a-priori" principle, namely the value of trying to realize value, "of discovering the possibilities of the actual and trying to realize them". In other words, there must be some "metaphysical charter for experiment", embodying a conviction that the universe makes the struggle worthwhile.[27] To use James' terms, Hocking feels that belief in an eternal absolute is really the presupposition of "tough-minded" investigation rather than a weakness of "tender-mindedness".

The quasi-experimental method to which Hocking turns has much in common with the dialectical method illustrated by Plato and formalized by Hegel. "Leaving Hegel's result out of account, we may recognize in his idea of a 'synthesis', as something quite different from an addition of heterogeneous truths, the sort of relation among partial truths which we desire as the eventual principle of our philosophy to hold". Such a principle would seek to do "full justice to the empirical and experimental genius of our age, while recognising, as empiricism does not, that the last truth in the order of discovery may well be a *necessary* truth. . . . The final success of the inductive method is the uncovering of necessary or a priori truth."[28] Indeed, induction is in a sense circular, he claims, in that through it there is continuously "rediscovered", in progressively sharper outline, the true premises which define the area of its operations.[29]

So Hocking's philosophic method may be called an "empirical dialectic", operating at all times with an element of fixed certainty in tension with "an ingredient of hypothesis". Such a dialectic, he believes, differs from both Hegel's "pseudo-deductive dialectic" and from Dewey's "experimental pragmatism". "It is, I suggest, the union of their valid elements."[30]

This dialectical method is obviously bound up with the kind of religious experience which Hocking has stressed in his analysis of natural knowledge. It is because of the religious experience of the Whole, in detachment from and "running ahead" of part-experience, that the tension between certainty and uncertainty is possible. Indeed, the development of scientific and experimental method in Western culture, he maintains, was made possible by the ages of Stoic and Christian "detachment", and the "true result of the Western experiment, as I read it, is that detachment and attachment somehow belong together. . . . The enthusiasm with which the methods of science were worked out and the laws of nature conceived and verified was a direct consequence of that long prior restraint."[31] Fruitful inductive method, like reflection in general, derives its pattern from a religious search for certainty;

> Every induction is *induced* by a prior induction . . . , or judgment about the whole of things—none other than my whole-idea, derived from whatever knowledge of the whole and of God my experience has built up for me. Every induction is at the same time a deduction, then,—an "It must be so" parented, though from the background of consciousness, by an insight which in its origins is essentially religious.[32]

So Hocking maintains that religion is the womb of scientific method, the "parent of the arts"; thus scientific approaches to religion are themselves dependent upon a prior and basic religious commitment.

This brings to the fore again a feature of Hocking's conception of religious knowledge which must be stressed if his conception of philosophic method is to be understood; namely that for him God as the Whole is an object of certain experience, and not a metaphysical hypothesis. Hypothetical belief in God is worthless, he feels; only certain knowledge qualifies for commitment and devotion. The certainty of the experience of the Whole makes possible the free and experimental character of scientific method itself. Thus it must again be asked whether there is such an experiential certainty of "evolving" reality, a certainty which is "in tension" with the uncertainties of unfinished experience. Or is this notion of certainty not itself a "regulative ideal", a co-implicate of tentative experience, perhaps, rather than an overt item of that experience? And it may also be asked whether the operationalists whom he criticizes actually neglect the "dialectical" character of experiment, in practice. Certainly none of them would deny that what has been found to be true in scientific inquiry is, in a sense, "forever" true—under the conditions and in the context in which it was established. What they have insisted upon is the possibility and probability of broadening contexts and the emergence of new data as time goes on. It may be that there is a certain "timeless" character of purely formal "truths" such as those of mathematics and certain types of logic. And it would seem that this is actually the type of truth which Hocking has in mind when he speaks of theoretical certainty. But he may hardly claim to have taken fully seriously the significance of the particular and the contingent, with which the natural sciences, at least, are concerned, when he insists upon a theoretical rather than a "practical" certainty in the whole field of scientific inquiry. Idealists like Brightman and Boodin, as we shall see, do attempt to take these factors seriously and find their systems considerably modified as a consequence.

Hocking's belief that scientific inquiry must be based upon a kind of timeless certainty has its counterpart also in his view of the relation of God to good and evil. In the field of ethical struggle only a type of monism can lead to a genuinely optimistic outlook, he believes. Though "no one can doubt that evil is evil", nevertheless a radical pluralism or even an ultimate dualism in this respect is impossible; "there must be a unity in overcoming evils", such that overcoming makes a difference to the Whole. "No man", he writes, "can be content to accept evil as finality; each must have his *theory of evil,* as a means of bringing that evil under the conception of the whole, and so . . . of disposing of it". Evil, in other words, is "transmutable"; apparent evils are seen to be goods in broader contexts, and experience reveals that pain can be "overcome" in courageous devotion to a certain cause. The "untransmuted" evils of a "closed life" are ultimate only if one assumes that no absolute mind exists, which, in its timeless perspective, creates a moral continuity beyond the present and the apparent. This view should not lead to any lessening of moral effort, Hocking believes; choices in time are real choices, and ethical decisions and activities "make a difference" in the Whole. Even the hope of immortality—or "immortability"—cannot reasonably or ethically be a hope for release from all struggle.[33] Nevertheless, if the struggle is to be worthwhile we must believe that the Real is the Good, and that evil is somehow "less real". No optimism can "take evil straight"; It must rather be based upon a clear and satisfying view of the Whole, in its infinite past and future, whose reality is ultimately good.[34] God, then, is "moral" as "He-Who-is". It is only as One beyond good and evil that He can transmute evil into good, as the all-powerful One whose "sun shines upon the just and the unjust". Genuine triumph over evil is to be found in an "association which cannot be corrupted", with an "Other-than-all-men", through whom pain and evil are seen "from the outside". God is the "Tao", the "still, small voice".[35]

Other empirical idealists who attempt to take more seriously the reality of time and the finality of concrete struggle differ radically from Hocking with respect to this crucial issue, as we shall see. Since we believe that, from a thoroughgoing empirical point of view, their criticisms are valid, we shall not introduce at this point further reflections. In coming to grips with this problem Brightman is led to his view of a "finite" God, while Hocking wrote, with respect to earlier statements of a similiar position, that "the finite God is of no worth".[36] Boodin, on the other hand, believes a thoroughgoing dualism to be more consistent with the "empirical" data, while others would agree that a genuinely "tough-minded" empiricism would accept a pluralism.

With reference to another question which some empirical philosophers of religion find debatable, Hocking maintains that God is experienced as personal. Though "we may find the thought of God following in arrear of the best conception we have of ourselves", we may realize that "it is only because we know that whatever selfhood we have is an involution of the selfhood of the Whole, and that our external relations to our fellows do but follow and reproduce in their own more distant form the relation of God to us which from His view is internal". However, it must be realized that the term "personality" as applied to God cannot have its usual rigid connotation; one must have in mind the vast living law and order of the universe, though personality "is a stronger concept than law". What is certain is that God is *experienced* as personal, as responsive to personal need and as the bearer of companionship. But to say that God is personal is by no means to say that He is in any sense "finite"; the experience and companionship of God are not in competition with human alliances.[37]

It may be of interest to indicate briefly the manner in which Hocking applies his empirical dialectic to problems of conduct and history. Like other empiricists in this field, he is critical of a purely rationalistic deduction of a hierarchy of transcendent values dissociated from the concrete realm of facts. He cannot, however, accept the view that values are themselves "facts" in any simple sense of the term. Though men are concretely concerned with local and "spotwise values", and all ethical analysis must take this basic consideration into account, the "illusion of local values" as final leads dialectically to the discovery that such values are not stable but change with social contexts and personal relations. There is, he believes, a "general principle of relativity in regard to values", to the effect that all goodness is goodness for a self; but this also means that any particular good is always a case of "a total right-relation between the enjoyer and his world". This, in turn, leads to the perception of the "concrete objectivity" of an "absolute good", the latter being defined in terms of the interpenetration of values and the integration of the self entertaining them. The "absolute good" is not a perfectly realised realm apart from the world of ethical striving. But dealing with facts alone leads to a realization of the objectivity of ideals, just as any intelligent concern for ideals must be related to means for their concrete realization in the realm of fact. Ideals are in part discoveries and not mere inventions of the imagination, as some empiricists have held. An ideal, in brief, may be "in" the world of fact as a partial realization; but it is also in "tension" with the world of partial realizations. "The divine nature is at odds with every particular it inhabits; the essence of the good is dissatisfied with its actual garb and struggles beyond its integument." Thus man's idealizing is neither a defiant "free-man's worship" nor a striving after values which have only an imaginary status before their realization, but rather

> an attempt to decipher the inward driving and straining force, the intension of things. . . . The locus of what we call "reality" shifts from the particular facts toward this concrete entity, the process of the world as *an intended labor*. Thus in contemplating "the good" we contemplate "the real" as well. . . . Our normal detachment is first of all our effort to discern this concretely objective "will of the world", the God who is critic and alterer and not alone the conservative substance at the center of the world.[38]

Thus in his treatment of values and ideals Hocking tries again to combine the insights of empirical ethical analysis with certain emphases more traditionally associated with rationalistic and transcendental treatments. Other empirical religious philosophers, as we shall see, seek to avoid the transcendentalism implied by Hocking, with varying degrees of success. Professor Wieman in particular denies even the relative distinction upon which Hocking insists with reference to fact and value, and is led thereby to the position that God is rather a perceptible fact of nature. As for this latter question of whether or not "nature" is a suitable category in which to speak of fact and value, world and God, Hocking has lately indicated that the matter is not, for him, one of primary concern. It is true that he has vigorously attacked what he terms "the illicit naturalising of religion, and has offered extended critiques of the older mechanistic and materialistic naturalisms which overlook the rôle of mind and value in reality. H rejects any program which would substitute for what has been called "th supernatural" that which is only analogous to it, or represents its effects i action. He is particularly concerned to point out that the act of worshi "directs attention beyond all misleading secular momenta, effecting di continuity in the entire physical and social circumstance of thought".[39]

However, he recognizes the fact that the term "naturalism" has som times been used in recent thought with such broad connotations as to mak room for most of the values for which the "supernatural" has stood. Th apparent "religiousness of our time", the "passion for righteousness an duty", the recognition of "the good of the struggle"; these and other fa tors suggest, he believes, that "the meanings which were once associate with the term 'supernatural' are being recovered for social use, and as were naturalised. . . . Whether we speak of supernature, or simply of shift which has taken place in the position of 'nature' is not of primary in portance".[40]

Returning, then, to some illustrations of the manner in which ou philosopher has applied his empirical dialectic to socio-ethical and politi cal problems, to which he has devoted considerable attention,[41] it shoul be pointed out that one significant basis for such analyses has been his vie of the human self as an "empirical duality", irreducible to either th "body" or to the "mind" of traditional dualisms. It is not simply "body with reference to space and time, being related, through "mind", to thes categories in ways significantly different from those in which mindle bodies are. Nor is it fruitful to view the self in terms of its mental chara teristics, as if these were not intricately and inextricably bound up wi the physical. Rather the self is a unity, "a system of purposive behavi emerging from a persistent hope". The mind "needs" a body as its "met phor" for its individuation, as "a visible object to which I can refer certa wants and powers and my steady sense of being, here and now", as the i strument of will through which future purposes are presently expressib and as the instrument of "give-and-take" with nature and other selves. I such activity the total self is "free" by virtue of its "freedom of attentio and its freedom of self-determination in terms of adopted goals.[42]

In a similar manner he has offered a dialectical interpretation of th relation of individual selves to society, maintaining that recent emphas upon the social character of human existence have afforded, some of the through exaggerated distortions of half-truths, a needed corrective f some of the shortcomings of classical liberalism. He believes that the

will emerge as a result a new appreciation of the significance of the social
orientation of the individual, but that at the same time the failure of col-
lectivisms will lay bare in clear perspective "the lasting elements of individualism".[43]

In a broader analysis he writes that history reveals that man continuously acts upon the intuitive certainty that he knows what he wants to be,
and that he must constantly "remake" himself in order to reach his goal.
In doing this he fashions a number of life-hypotheses, attempts to fulfill
them, and subjects them to revision. "The process itself always follows the
same shape, which in its simplest expression is like that of an inductive
science."[44] But the nature of human nature and its true goal is not empirically discoverable; to think that it is, is to confuse the goal with material. The scientific study of man as a social organism affords only the
basis for experiment. Looking "outward" and "forward" raises problems
of value and standards, and suggests an "ultimate court which gives laws
to nature, rather than receiving laws from nature."[45] A dialectical analysis
of individual "instincts" and social ideals suggests that an essentially
democratic conception of society is most fruitful; but social norms are
derived ultimately from "private" norms, which must have a trans-social
and "objective" frame of reference. Religion must supply these absolutes.

And it is Christianity which most clearly supplies the norms for the ideal
society, because it recognizes the significance of individuality and ambition while transforming it into the "passion for souls" which results in the
historic spread of the Beloved Community. Its center of loyalty is, in a
sense, "beyond this world", but it demands action "in the world".[46] Such
an ideal fulfills the "dialectic of experience" because of its concrete historicity in one institution among others, slowly permeating the life of society in the interest of "world culture and international law".[47]

But the reality of the Christian concept of God and its world-view must
be factual and not hypothetical. "The question, How is love to God or to
men possible if as a fact I do not have it? would be answered if there were,
as the moving spirit of the world, an aggressive lover able and disposed to
break in upon my temper of critical egoism and win my response".[48] The
Christian God is such; He is the Seeker, acting and suffering in history.
Thus the question whether such a view of the world be true is not to be
answered in terms of one "hypothesis" among others; no substitute "élan
vital" or "finite God" will do; "it is a question of fact".[49]

Now Hocking frankly admits that to see the dialectic of human experience fulfilled in the Christian ideal is "retrospective". This means that
something has appeared

as a positive datum, something personally experienced or "revealed." It

is here that religion takes the issue out of the hands of philosophy. For
religion in its historical forms is empirical; it appeals to the realistic
temper: it deals with facts. Its function is not to prove God but to an-
nounce Him . . . it appeals only to man's power to *recognize what he
needs in what is real.* Hence religion calls upon every man for an individual and ultimate "I believe" which means . . . "I see."[50]

This insight is rather significant, in view of certain questions which we
wish to raise later regarding other empirical approaches to religion. The
ultimate and personal quality of religious decision is seen by him to "take
the issue out of the hands of philosophy"; he frankly recognizes the
primacy of Christian insight for his own system. Others are more am
biguous on this score. However, in considering the problem of a world
faith, Hocking rejects what he calls the "way of radical displacement"
through which one religion with particular cultural roots of its own would
displace others. Religion cannot become universal in the same way tha
science may; it is more akin to art, which is bound up with local cultura
expressions. On the other hand, the reductionist ideal of a liberalism which
would achieve a loose synthesis of the "best" of all faiths in one is also
undesirable. Rather the "way of reconception" must be followed, employ
ing the broad method of empirical dialectic. There should be an attempt

> to discern the substance of the matter underlying all this profusion o
> religious expression, to apprehend the generating principle of religious
> life and of each particular form of it[51]—

the universal element which is intuited by each religion from its own per
spective. This process would reveal, he believes, a "growth within same
ness", through a succession of hypotheses about a changeless truth. And
that faith which, in friendly rivalry and intercommunication with others
could prove most capable of expressing the deeper insights of all, would
become the world-faith. Hocking believes that Christianity in its *idea*
expression may well afford the basis for such a faith as is needed by moder
man. It has developed free thought, free social applications, and a meaning
for "the common man"; it "may readily be described as the embodied an
clarified anticipation, by some two thousand years, of these very convic
tions to which the grasping soul of man . . . slowly turns". But Chri
tianity as embodied in existing institutions is not yet ready to serve as
world-faith, because it has not solved certain problems concerning th
bearing of its faith upon certain crucial social problems, and because it :
still too often bound up with extraneous features of Western culture.[52]

Our summary account of Hocking's religious philosophy has reveale
several modifications of absolutism as a result of empirical emphases. I

his general view of experience he seeks to take account of affective and volitional as well as of rational factors, and he insists upon the significance of the particular, concrete, and contingent in the knowledge-situation. With reference to the specific problem of religious knowledge, he seeks to show that a type of religious referent is implied in all knowledge of nature and society, and also that there is one kind of religious experience, namely the mystical, which offers at the same time an empirical basis for knowledge of God and a necessary foundation for the fruitful and consistent use of scientific method in natural and social inquiry. His version of such method, described in terms of empirical dialectic, seeks to do full justice to the tentative and open character of experience as interpreted by science.

Similarly, in his approach to problems of conduct and history, he takes into consideration the concrete "spotwise" values which are empirically discovered in an ethical analysis of human behavior and the significance of particular and changing social patterns and cultural contexts. His awareness of the role of particular cultural patterns in the development and expression of religious faiths leads him to reject both the traditional "way of radical displacement" and the reductionistic liberal "way of synthesis" in the approach to the problem of a world faith. In these and other respects his thought reflects what may be described as an empirical temper, as he turns to concrete experience and a form of empirical method in his understanding of central problems.

Nevertheless, we have found that his interpretation of what is "given" in natural and social experience involves notions which, we belive, may be more accurately described as rationalistic and subjectivistic rather than empirical. We have suggested that a lingering psychologism is at least in part responsible for his positing the existence of "Other Mind" in order to "explain" natural and social experience, and that this same subjectivism is reflected in his insistence upon the significance of "knowledge of the Whole". Similarly, his belief that affective and volitional elements in experience are significant only as materials for rational cognition, and that any understanding of the particular and contingent presupposes a rational conception of "the whole", reflects an essentially rationalistic ideal. His "discovery" of God in natural and social knowledge is, in turn, bound up with these presuppoitions, as is his defense of the ontological argument as "empirical". As for his evaluation of mystical experience as affording certain and normative religious knowledge, we have raised various questions concerning the relationship of theory to experience in a position of this kind, and have suggested that a more empirical view of religious experience would have to take more seriously the significance of divergent forms.

We have sought further to show that his supplementation of that type of scientific inquiry, which could perhaps with less ambiguity be termed empirical, with his concept of empirical dialectic, seems not to be warranted by an examination of scientific inquiry itself, but rather to rest, again, on certain rationalistic notions expressed in terms of the religious quest for certainty. A similar strain of "tender-mindedness" is seen, we believe, in his belief that an adequate interpretation of empirical values in conduct leads necessarily to belief in a kind of transcendental ideal. This strain is reflected even more clearly in his treatment of evil and his belief that a type of ethical monism is the only sound basis for ethical optimism. And, finally, whereas he seeks to do justice to the significance of plurality and particularity in culture and religion, his application of empirical dialectic in these areas leads him to the belief that there is a single definable goal towards which all cultures are moving, and that a particular historical religion may, at least in its "ideal form", become the world-faith. In these respects he consciously abandons a more strictly empirical approach, having offered from time to time extended criticisms of that type of experimentalism which we believe to be, historically and logically, the clearest modern expression of the empirical tradition. Other idealists have been led to abandon some of the positions held by Hocking in their attempts to develop an empirical religious philosophy; we turn now to a further examination of two systems which illustrate some of the alternative positions possible within an idealistic framework.

II: E. S. Brightman, *Personalistic Idealist*

Edgar Sheffield Brightman (b. 1884) was born and raised in the home of a New England Methodist minister where, as he writes, he was "subjected to unceasing religious influences from the start". Though the general tenor of his religious background was what modern American Protestants would call "conservative", he believes that a considerable emphasis upon the ethical implications of evangelical Christianity in his home preserved him from "practical illiberalism". His early interests were varied; he lists "camp-meetings, Darwin, Greek, and psychic phenomena" as being among topics of youthful investigation. He received his undergraduate college training at Brown, where he devoted considerable attention to philosophy, while continuing his study of Darwinian scientific theory, Greek, and "argumentation". Among philosophers who claimed his first attention were Plato, Marcus Aurelius, Epictetus, Berkeley, and Nietzsche; later he was attracted by Kant and Schopenhauer. But his "first real allegiance" in philosophy, he says, was to Royce's idealism, which he "accepted as a whole for two or three years"

Then, during a period of graduate study, he read James' *Pragmatism* which, as he puts it, "swept him off his feet"; he became and remained for a time an ardent disciple of James. But later, when some one gave him "a pat illustration of a useful and successful error", he was led to reject certain important features of James' doctrine as he understood it, and he has remained "permanently critical of pragmatism in all its forms". Rather he found in the personalistic teachings of B. P. Bowne, at Boston University, a philosophical position which seemed to him to "combine the truth that there was in James and Royce with a criticism of the errors of each". He has subsequently come to modify some of Bowne's positions in his own philosophy, primarily as a result of what he terms "a greater attention to empirical fact". Among other things he has placed more emphasis upon the idea of evolution, and has found in Hegel "a more concrete and adequate view of reason". Thus, like Hocking, Brightman has sought to express a persisting religious interest in terms of a philosophy embodying both absolutistic and pragmatic influences and elements.[1]

"Experience", he writes, "is the necessary starting point of any philosophy of religion".[2] No adequate religious philosophy can overlook any of the facts of experience, and the conclusions reached by the philosopher of religion must be judged in terms of their relevance to experience. Furthermore, the method which he employs in establishing his conclusions must reflect the character of the experience which it seeks to interpret and must be akin, "at least in spirit" to the procedures of scientific inquiry. In other words, a valid religious philosophy, according to Brightman, must be definitely empirical in character. And he believes that if it is truly empirical it will also be personalistic and idealistic.

Now we have seen that when a philosopher seeks to base his conclusions upon the "facts of experience", much depends upon what he takes "experience" to be. This is clearly true in the case of a philosopher like Brightman, and therefore we must devote some attention to this problem at the outset, before proceeding to examine some of the specific views embraced in his religious philosophy as such. "Our experience", he says, "consists of our entire conscious life", and "religion is one phase of our experience". Philosophy of religion, accordingly, "is the experience of interpreting those experiences which we call religious and of relating them to other experiences, as well as to our conception of experience as a whole".[3] Experience in general includes

the whole field of consciousness, every process or state of awareness in it; not sensation alone, not scientifically interpreted experience alone. It is not to be taken in contrast with reason or speculation, but with the absence of experience. It is *Erlebnis*, not the Kantian *Erfahrung* alone. Experience is always complex, ongoing activity; thought and will belong to it as truly as do sensations and memory images. Hence, in the broad sense in which we use it, experience contains both what have been called empirical and what have been called transcendental (rational) factors.[4]

In other words, Brightman wishes the word "experience" to be understood in the broadest possible sense.

However, he believes that it can be so understood only if it be "synonymous with consciousness".[5] "Whatever is present in consciousness is said to be experienced; what at any given time is not present in consciousness is not experienced. The individual experiences his experience, lives his consciousness".[6] The *basic* experience is the experience of one's own consciousness; all else is inferred. This, he believes, is a cardinal fact "for one who is inclined to approach problems empirically": all "situations experienced" must be actually present in consciousness, and "the only situation experienced by anyone is his own consciousness."[7] Thus Brightman, while insisting upon an all-inclusive view of experience, a view which would include both "what has been called transcendental" and "what has been called empirical" elements in the same general category and which leads, as we shall see, to a corresponding inclusiveness in his understanding of "empirical method", at the same time stresses the significance of the subject in experience so strongly that he is led to equate experience with consciousness. This conception, in turn, has far-reaching consequences for his entire philosophical position, and especially for his philosophy of religion.

One such consequence is seen in his general analysis of the problem of knowledge, which in turn bears directly upon certain features of his theistic argument. He agrees with Dewey in making a distinction between experience and knowledge; the reference of any immediate experience to a supposed knowledge-object is called by him a "knowledge-claim". "It is never so certain that we know any object as it is that we are now conscious". And that of which we are immediately conscious, in the "specious present" is called the "datum-self". Any knowledge of the "Whole-self", including knowledge of its own past experience and its physical body, as well as its natural, social, and "spiritual" environments, is never more than inferred. The "datum-self" is described by Brightman as "more unified" than James' "stream of consciousness" but broader in scope than Royce's "span of consciousness", and as similar to Whitehead's "actual occasion" and Dewey's "situation", though the latter would include what Brightman calls "situations believed-in".[9] Any "situation experienced", then, is a "self, a person, or an experient, because it is a self-experiencing whole which includes thinking, choosing, remembering, anticipating, and purposing, as well as feeling and sensing . . . all bodies, brains, and gods are objects of belief."[10]

A "self" is defined by Brightman as "any and every consciousness, however simple or complex it may be. A self is a conscious situation experienced as a whole".[11] It is to be contrasted with "person", which is defined as "a self that is potentially self-conscious, rational, and ideal". He believes that "there is no good reason on the basis of known evidence to draw the line sharply and say that only human beings are persons; pigs, dogs, apes, and horses seem to be at least elementary persons". In any event, he believes that "self-experience, if not reflective self-consciousness, extends to the lowest forms of animal life". Though "to conceive the consciousness of a protozoan passes all our imagination; yet there is good reason to believe that every living being experiences itself as a self".[12] The difference between selves and persons, then is the difference between "any and every consciousness . . . each 'empirical situation' " and situations which are characterized by self-consciousness, rationality, and motivation by ideals. Selves exhibit a degree of spatio-temporal transcendence in a limited "specious present", some purposiveness, and some kind of "privacy", though not necessarily with awareness of it. Persons exhibit a more complex self-consciousness, the influence of moral, aesthetic, and religious values, a more extended "specious present", free purposive self-control, conceptual thought and reason, response to social and spiritual environments, and an awareness of privacy exhibited in a need to communicate.[13]

Now we have stated Brightman's views with reference to the nature of selves and persons in some detail because, according to him,

> this radically empirical point of view, which takes my personality to be my consciousness, is also a religious point of view, for religion is concerned with man's conscious experience of values, with man's spirit, with religious experience. The goal of religion is the development of worthy consciousness.[14]

Furthermore, his basic contention that all experience must be experience of a self or person is of fundamental importance in his argument for belief in a Cosmic Person as the experiencer of all reality. It may thus also be appropriate at this point to raise certain questions concerning these basic views. The fundamental question, of course, is whether Brightman is justified in his contention that the original experience is an experience of one's own consciousness, one's self. In holding this view Brightman seems to have reverted to the subjectivistic and individualistic assumptions of early British empiricism, though he has broadened the initial "datum" of experience to include some organization, volition, purpose, and so on. Nevertheless, there is the same assumption that the experient is himself somehow the most significant fact in his own experience, which assumption leads to the problem of how to "get outside" one's own immediate consciousness to external objects, which include one's own physical body and, according to Brightman, even one's past consciousness. Now even if it were granted that "experience" is intelligible only as involving experi*ents* of some sort, it would not seem to follow, necessarily, that what the experient experiences immediately can only be himself, the experient, or his own experienc*ing*. The position held by Brightman and other idealists who persist in what has been called the "psychologistic fallacy" seems to rest largely upon a confusion of the experient, experienc*ing*, and the experienc*ed*. Is it any more possible to conceive of an experient apart from something experienc*ed* by him, which is *not* simply his experienc*ing* of it, than it is to conceive of something experienc*ed* which is not the experience of some experient? If there are "subjective" elements in experience then there must of necessity be "objective" elements with independent and contrasting status, in terms of which the subjective is meaningful as such. Or, to put it in Brightman's terms, if "consciousness" is to be meaningful there must be some object of consciousness which is not itself consciousness; it is difficult to know what "consciousness of consciousness" could possibly signify. Empirically, consciousness seems to be as much "dependent" upon unconscious objects for its "existence" as such objects are, in a sense, "dependent" upon consciousness for their being *known*. Here, again, appears the confusion of knowing and being. It would seem that Brightman, though he holds a conception of experience which is in some respects all-inclusive, is definitely *un*empirical when, in what appears to be a confusion in the analysis of the knowledge-situation, he insists upon equating experience with consciousness. Empirically, consciousness seems rather to be one element *in* certain kinds of experience. For, even though "experience" implies experients, there seems to be no good reason for holding that affective and other elements are not truly experience until they emerge in consciousness, and much less reason for holding that the original "datum", epistemological or ontological, of experience is simply the experient.

This leads to the further question as to whether Brightman is justified in describing the basic type of experience as a datum-*self*. The question is one of definition, of course, and in such matters terms may be used arbitrarily. But it does seem questionable to use the same term to refer both to the "experience" or "consciousness" of protozoa and to the "experience" of complex animals or men. Empirically, the observable behavioral and functional patterns exhibit considerable differences. And the distinction between "self" and "person" would seem, on this basis, to be even more questionable. If the same term is used to describe both protozoa and higher animals, then it is not apparent why a different term is necessary at any point in the scale; if there be a distinction between selves and persons, then there would seem to be ample evidence for making a further distinction between selves and not-selves in the order of experience. In any event, it is not clear, as we have suggested above why the "datum-self" is of any more significance either in the knowledge-situation or in "existence" as such, than is the "whole-self" and its environment. Even if it were granted that the "datum-self" is *temporally* prior in the order of *cognition,* it would not necessarily follow that it is of primal significance in the general order of experience or nature. Yet many important features of Brightman's metaphysics and religious philosophy rest, at least in part, upon his analysis of experience as consciousness and his insistence upon the primacy of self or person in it.

As was suggested above, this type of analysis leads to a view of the "problem of knowledge" as the problem of the relation of the datum-self which is immediately experienced to the whole-self or person and the objects in its environment. This problem Brightman would solve in terms of a kind of epistemological dualism, because, if his definition of experience be accepted, not to go "beyond" experience is to end in solipsism—indeed, this is the position to which he believes positivists are driven. But there is *in* the experience of the "datum-self", he says, a reference beyond, demanded by the necessity of a field for its action and for a rational explanation of the changes experienced in the initial datum. External objects are thus "principles of explanation" of experience. And "truth" is to be understood as "agreement between subject and object", that is, between the immediately experienced subject and the object to which its experience seems to refer. However, though Brightman *defines* truth in terms of "correspondence", he cannot accept the correspondence-theory as affording an adequate *criterion* of truth, since we could not know that there is an actual correspondence between subject and object unless the object could be directly "given" in experience. And, according to him, ideas can be "compared" only with each other, never with "things" (Locke).[15]

Rather he turns to what he calls "coherence" as affording the only criterion of truth. "Coherence" is a logical criterion, embracing both deductive and inductive types of logical inquiry. It signifies, he says, "systematic consistency", the "sticking-together of a comprehensive, synoptic-view of experience". According to this criterion, any judgment is true, if it is both self-consistent and coherently connected with our system of judgments as a whole". If reason be defined as "the power of testing truth-claims by logical and empirical standards, the principles of induction and deduction, and, above all, the perception of the relations between parts and wholes", then "coherence" may be described simply as "the principle of reason".[16] It should be noted that Brightman does not use the term in the strictly logical sense of Bradley. "Rational experience . . . means inclusive, consistent, orderly experience. It does not mean the experience of incessant reflection on logic and mathematics . . . perpetual syllogising . . . or a state of continuous doubt or scepticism". And, as we shall see, the wholly "coherent" account of experience must take account of the "irrational" and "meaningless" as well.[17]

We shall have occasion later to raise certain questions about the employment of this broad notion of "coherence" as a criterion of truth, in connection with its role in "empirical method". We are ready to turn now to some of the more specifically religious questions to which he has given considerable attention, with our analysis of his general view of experience and truth as a background which may illuminate to some extent the conclusions which he reaches in this connection.

Essentially the same form of analysis appears in his view of religious experience and its knowledge-value. Though he agrees with other empirical religious philosophers that ǁapart from experience, there is no basis for belief in the goodness, the purposiveness, or the intelligence of the world-groundǀ and apart from specifically religious experience there is no basis for belief in a specifically religious realityǁ,[18] nevertheless he cannot agree with Hocking and others that any one type of religious experience is self-authenticating or normative. He prefers, rather, to define religious experience broadly as "any experience of any person taken in relation to his God".[19] He is appreciative of various types of phenomena which could fall within this classification but refuses to take any specific form as determinative. Meditation, prayer, mystical insight, religiously motivated activity in society in the interest of ideals—all of these may be religious experiences. He accepts, in the main, Hocking's analysis of worship.[20] But he avoids the difficulties, suggested in the last Section, of holding that there is any kind of "pure" experience uncolored by the assumptions of the experient. "Pure" religious experience, he says,

> is an abstraction as unreal as "pure" sensation in psychology. Some mystics and empiricists in religion appear to have forgotten this fact. On the other hand, religious beliefs, apart from the experience out of which they grew and on which they are nourished are abstractions equally unreal.[21]

No single experience carries its truth with it; all must be tested in terms of "coherence" and synoptic insight into experience as a whole.[22]

The essential nature of religious experience then consists in an "appeal to the largest and most inclusive view of experience". The function of religion is "to relate each moment to the meaning and purpose of the whole universe". Thus, while specific religious experiences cannot be used alone as evidence of the object towards which they point, they may, when taken in connection with the total world-view derived from a coherent interpretation of all experience be regarded as "strong empirical confirmation of the belief in God".[23] The thesis that religious experience affords an autonomous source of knowledge and the antithesis that it is completely reducible to non-religious factors are resolved in the synthetic proposition that religious experience when critically interpreted may make significant contributions to the whole of knowledge. Taking the mass of phenomena labelled "religious experience" as the "datum", one should turn to the descriptive sciences of religion for detailed analysis of the subject-matter. One is thus led to seek the "empirical cause" of the phenomena, which science, limited to description, cannot apprehend. The question then raised by the "datum" is thus "Of what data ideally inaccessible to me is my datum the sign?", which, as in the broader problem of knowledge in general, involves the further question "Of what logical implications is my datum the sign?"[24] and, finally, "Of what values" and "Of what total universe". These questions, in turn, are to be investigated through the use of empirical method.

Now we have said that his conception of empirical method is bound up with the idea of coherence as a criterion of truth. "Coherence is no repudiation of empiricism. It is simply an insistence that empiricism must be complete, well-ordered, clearly defined, and rationally interpreted".[25] In his earlier writings he called his method of investigation "synoptic" and characterized it as the method which includes the insights of rationalistic and scientific methods, as well as appeals to "intuition", by "viewing any object or complex of objects as a whole".[26] Scientific method alone, he claimed, is limited to a descriptive function; it cannot and should not attempt evaluations. Philosophy of religion, using the synoptic or empirical method, is to evaluate the specific findings of the sciences of religion. At present it must also "evaluate the evaluations" of certain sciences which, in claiming to be "normative", make unwarranted metaphysical assertions.[27]

The question of theistic belief is thus viewed as basically a metaphysical issue, involving the question whether there be "a unity or harmony between existence and value". And, since scientific verification usually points ostensively to a particular public object or set of objects, whereas a proposition about God is not primarily concerned with tangible and public "things", therefore the empirical method employed in investigating the truth of the theistic hypothesis is not strictly scientific. God cannot be defined ostensively; thus there can be no crucial experiments for the verification of the theistic hypothesis.

> God is not an object visible to the senses, and his existence is not capable of experimental verification in any such sense as is a scientific hypothesis about the physical world. . . . It is true that an experimental attitude may and should be taken toward belief in God; but the experiment of testing the reality of God by trying to find him through every avenue of our being is very different in many respects from a strictly scientific experiment under precisely-controlled physical conditions. I believe that Professor Henry Nelson Wieman, for all his earnestness and intelligent sincerity, has exaggerated the scientific nature of religious knowledge.[28]

This criticism we must consider when we examine in more detail the theory mentioned.

But, while rejecting the idea that empirical verification of God is of the same pattern as scientific method, Brightman holds that there are certain similarities between the two. All verifications must begin and end in some person's present experience, and each kind of verification is "a type of system." Purpose, insight, and fact are all presupposed in any kind of verification, and all results must be "synoptically apprehended". On the other hand, both scientific and metaphysical verification are limited in their conclusions to hypothetical propositions. This is the great insight of modernity which forces a revision of the Cartesian-Spinozistic goal, he believes. No process of verification could be called complete until all experience has ended.[29] To say that something is true "once for all" is really to make a hypothetical judgment that it *would* be so acknowledged by competent observers who possessed all the evidence, and all the evidence is not forthcoming at any point in time. Beyond this specific limitation of certainty there is the more basic assumption, which is really an hypothesis, that the universe as such is rational. And, for Brightman, there is also the further hypothesis, with respect to all truth, that it applies to a "reality" which is not given in the immediate experience from which it is derived.[30] However, reality never totally evades our certain grasp when we realize that we as experients are part of it. And "theoretical relativism" in all spheres may be coupled with a "practical absolutism"; one may *act* absolutely on the strength of the supposition that a belief is true until it has been proved false. In this connection Brightman says that he "feels a kinship" with James and Dewey.[31]

And so the experimental method with which Brightman approaches the problem of religious truth, though different from scientific method in scope, seeks to preserve "the scientific spirit of quest and integrity". Whereas science investigates facts and laws of nature and devises instruments and means of control, religion seeks, in the same spirit, ultimate standards of value.[32] "Both science and philosophy are movements of experience from a state of confusion toward a state of order and coherence. Science is such a movement in a limited field; philosophy aims to interpret all experience in a comprehensive unity. . . . One who holds [this] viewpoint is called an empiricist."[33] Though there is no valid appeal to "a prioris" apart from experience, in religion, because all axioms or postulates must be thought about, and hence are, by definition, experienced; nevertheless, sense-experience alone patently is not value-experience, so the positivist errs as greatly as the "a priorist", but in the opopsite direction. A broader conception of experience and empirical method, however, is self-justifying; whereas apriorism would have to dispose of all other methods to establish itself and positivism would have to show that it rules out value-experience by definition:

> an empirical method . . . does not require that its field be cleared of all opponents, for the reason that it is so inclusive and liberal in its attitude as to find a place for all points of view, all types of belief, and even all objections to itself. The empirical method demands that the mind survey all the facts that have any bearing on the subject at hand; and this would include all competing theories too.[34]

Perhaps a clue to Brightman's change from "synoptic" to "empirical" in the designation of his method is to be seen in his coming to think of reason as a "function of experience". At one time he rejected "thoroughgoing empiricism" because, if experience is only the immediate experience of the 'datum-self", the empiricist must be a solipsist.[35] More recently he has said that reason and experience are not to be dichotomized, but that reason is a "function of experience" as "experience is a movement toward rational totality".[36] In this connection he writes that a "radical change" dominated his thinking in the decade 1929-39, "a change from emphasis on the rationalistic and *a priori* factors in religious knowledge to emphasis on the empirical". He now sees that empiricism may be more than Humian sensationism, and that pragmatic empiricism "is not so much false as incompletely empirical". In his broader conception he can view "liberalism and rationalism, properly understood" as "names for this empirical method".[37]

A major factor in this change of emphasis was a deeper acquaintance with Hegel, whom he describes as "the empiricist of consciousness". When Hegel declares that "the true is the whole", says Brightman, it is plain that he is thus the most thorough empiricist, the one who explores every nook and cranny of the spiritual life. . . . Hegel has led me to see that true rationalism is simply the principle of confronting every part of experience with our view of the whole, while true empiricism is the principle of accepting only that view of the whole which is honestly built up by observation of the acceptable parts of experience.[38]

Though Hegel erred in not seeing that the idea of *Geist* as an impersonal or superpersonal social mind, feeding upon its constituent persons, is less adequate empirically than a personalistic view, it is nevertheless clear that "the completer empiricism is idealism".[39]

Now the obvious question to be raised at this point is whether Brightman's shift from the more rationalistic synoptic method to what he now calls empirical method is really more than a redefinition of terms. In his earlier writings he thought of empiricism as being concerned primarily with sense-experience and so distinguished between empiricism and rationalism. But now he broadens the definition of experience, retaining at the same time the subjectivistic emphasis, and consequently accepts an empirical method which "is so inclusive and liberal in its attitude as to find a place for all points of view". It still embraces all the values of "liberalism and rationalism" as well as the specific emphases of experimental method. It includes apriorism because a prioris are "thought about" and hence empirical. But is not a method "so inclusive and liberal in its attitude" guilty of what Professor Loewenberg has referred to as the "fallacy of the suppressed correlative"?[40] When empirical method is equated with all the ways of the mind involved in inquiry it loses any specific connotation and makes alternative methods unthinkable. This procedure is not only confusing to those who have associated a more specific meaning with empirical method, but it is also a fruitless addition to philosophical terminology. Why should the whole enterprise of thought be called *a* method, when it admittedly includes *all* methods?

But Professor Brightman intends more than redefinition when he speaks of his shift from rationalism to empiricism. Perhaps the most significant consequence is actually the more definite abandonment of the rationalistic *ideal* of "finished" truth. Whereas Hocking admits the values of experimentalism, he still insists upon the relevance and possibility of "eternal truth" and certainty. Brightman agrees more fully with James and Dewey that, for one who takes time and the true nature of experimental verification seriously, the idea of eternal truth can at best be only "regulative". All truth is held by him to be hypothetical—except, perhaps, the "truth" that one is experiencing a given state of consciousness at a given moment. All propositions, including propositions about God, are seen to be constantly subject to revision or capable of achieving higher degrees of probability, though never certainty. This emphasis is more congenial to what has been called experimental method, and perhaps should be chiefly stressed by Brightman when he speaks of empiricism. But we must see whether the view of religious knowledge and its object held by him is at all points consistent with this type of emphasis. From the point of view of religious faith, it must be asked also whether the "practical certainty", of religious commitment, the commitment of "existential decision", is of one cloth with the practical certainty of scientific and metaphysical hypotheses which are subject both to momentary revision and to increase in probability as the testimony of controlled experiment mounts.

But if it be granted that the change in Brightman's thought which is most evidently "empirical" concerns the implications of experimental method, is he then justified in claiming that idealism is the only true empiricism? This would seem to hinge, again, upon his definition of experience as well as upon the "inclusive and liberal" character of his empirical method. Though he now includes in his understanding of the subject-matter of empiricism more than sensation, he still limits it to the "content of conscious awareness", and consequently holds that "reality" exists only "in, of, or for persons". If this be granted, then it is true that the only true empiricism would be an "empiricism of consciousness", for the only "real" subject-matter would be consciousness of some type. But again we must ask whether it follows from the fact that "reality" may be *known* only through conscious awareness that therefore consciousness is the only reality there is. The drawing of such an apparently unwarranted conclusion is one of the reasons why Brightman holds that there must be one supreme Person "in and for whose thought and will all physical things exist so that they are nothing apart from him",[41] and that "the universe is completely mental in nature".[42] Does it follow from the fact, if admitted, that "every item of experience belongs to a self", that experience or "reality" itself is personal?[43] We have already raised similar questions with respect to his analysis of knowledge, and we shall have occasion to reflect upon the metaphysical issues later in connection with some non-idealistic empiricisms. We only wish to point out here that it seemingly does *not* follow simply from the use of experimental *method* that empiricism must be idealistic, but that the basis for such a claim apparently lies in the conception of experience held by idealists, or else in such *non*-experimentalistic features of method as Brightman retains, like the "experienced" a prioris.

With reference to such a prioris, Brightman has written:

An empiricist would reply to an apriorist as follows: It is misleading to declare that there is anything independent of experience. The case of the apriorist derives its force from the indubitable fact that there is a difference in importance between four apples and two plus two equals four. The empiricist insists, however, that the process of thinking that two plus two equals four is as truly a conscious experience as is the process of observing four Macintosh Reds. The same is true of our thought regarding any axiom or postulate. . . . The trouble arises from using the word experience in a restricted meaning. . . . It is better to be a thoroughgoing empiricist and define experience as meaning all that is at any time present in consciousness. Thus the misunderstandings to which aprioris give rise are largely a matter of definition. . . . It is possible that some truths are universal and necessary; but this fact cannot be known prior to experiences of thinking and observing.[44]

Now Brightman indicates in other connections that he does not mean by this sort of redefinition that all of the views held by "apriorists" are thereby included in "empirical method".[45] But it would seem that to admit even the "apriorist" or rationalistic *ideal* into empirical method simply by definition is itself an illustration of "the harm done by inadequate definition". Historically and, it would seem, logically, empiricism is less ambiguously understood as an alternative to rationalism. And, in his conception of empirical method, Brightman does abandon *some* of the traditional rationalistic emphases, such as the ideal of "finished" and "certain" truth; he is aware of the fact that experience is "in the making".

But is not the "idea of the whole" which, as we have seen, plays such a large part in his entire philosophy, itself more definitely associated with rationalism than with empiricism? He has much to say about "truth as a whole", "reality as a whole", "experience as a whole", and so on. Are these "wholes" found *in* experience? It may indeed be true that each experient has some sort of awareness that his *own* experience constitutes a kind of "whole", psychologically speaking. But Brightman seems to mean more than this when he speaks of "the whole"; he means rather the *whole* of *unfinished* (!) experience, the whole of all knowledge, the "whole" of "reality". And it is not clear just when and where and how these appear in "experience", individual or collective. Such notions may, indeed, function as "regulative ideals", as has been suggested before, and it may be that Brightman means them to be understood simply in this sense, since as such they are sometime "in consciousness". But we maintain that a more thoroughgoing empiricism, which would limit itself to gross and public experience, would of necessity limit its knowledge-claims, even though they be hypothetical, to the directly verifiable realm of concrete, particular, plural "part"-experiences. To make assertions about the "ultimate" character of all experience and all truth involves rationalistic speculation which is not ordinarily associated with "empirical method".

Even so, when one bases his view of religious experience and truth upon their relation to the "reasonable" or "synoptic" view of all experience, or, more specifically, upon what to each particular investigator seems to be the "reasonable" interpretation of the "synoptic" view of all experience, he is introducing personal and subjective assumptions into the matter. By what criterion is one to determine when he has viewed all the relevant facts? By what criterion is he to determine which facts are relevant and which "synoptic" interpretation is correct—for in this realm there is a notorious plurality of interpretations of essentially the same facts! Some, upon examining the "evidence", may conclude that the theistic hypothesis best "explains" all the facts; others may arrive at quite different conclusions. And, among those who adopt theistic hypotheses, there may be and, as a matter of fact, is considerable disagreement as to just what kind of theism is demanded. And quite a number of different interpretations would seem to be equally "consistent" or "coherent", granted their basic assumptions. The issue then becomes a matter of speculative argument or personal conviction.

When what may be more accurately termed "empirical method" is employed, however, the appeal is to publicly available facts, and the hypotheses employed in the interpretation of su   facts, interpretation which takes full account of plurality and contingency in the data investigated, are of such a nature that they are open to public verification under definitely stated conditions. And we would maintain that it is the employment of investigation of this sort, the character of which we shall suggest in more detail later, which could most accurately and fruitfully constitute an empirical religious philosophy.

But a clearer notion of what Brightman means by the employment of empirical method with reference to the "theistic hypothesis" is seen in his analysis of value-experience in connection with its verification. We have seen that he conceives the essential problem of religious philosophy to be that of the relation of values to existence; therefore a major area of experience with which it is concerned is the realm of value-experience. Furthermore he believes that the experience of moral obligation is "a more immediate experience than is the existence of God" and that "the binding law of obligation and implied command to realize values do not depend logically or psychologically on belief in religion, and therefore the whole realm of religious experience rests on the basis of loyalty to moral obligation".[46]

Moral experience occurs whenever there is an experience of obligation, which is an irreducible category, or when there is a choice to be made between a "better" and a "worse". "Moral laws" are to be discovered in turn through the rational criticism and organization of moral experience.[47]

A "moral law" is defined as "a universal principle to which the will ought to conform in its choices". The rational criticism of moral experience which is to reveal moral laws involves the observation of value-experiences in general, a generalization of their similarities and conflicts, and a reinterpretation aimed at eliminating contradictions, with a final formulation of an inclusive hypothesis. This procedure is broadly empirical, though not scientific, because it is impossible to have moral experience under laboratory conditions and no series of experiments could establish a normative ethical law. As a result of such an analysis, Brightman has worked out a "system of moral laws", which we shall not enumerate here.[48]

This raises the question as to the nature and status of values and the ideals by which they are to be judged. Value he has defined as "whatever is liked, desired or approved" [49] "True value", as distinguished from value-in-general, is "what is liked, desired or approved in light of our whole experience and highest ideals".[50] Just as immediate cognitive experiences have only "knowledge-claim", so immediate value-experiences have only "value-claim". And the analysis of value-claims which reveals the nature of "true values" and the hierarchy of intrinsic as over against instrumental values hinges upon the ideals which are adopted as value-criteria. Ideals are defined as "concepts of what ought to be . . . hopes, promises, plans";[51] values are thus seen to be ideals realized or in process of realization.

And Brightman's interest in the analysis of ideals indicates that he takes "idealism" to mean, literally, the "philosophy of ideals". In an early volume he defended the thesis that ideals "reveal the objective structure, or perhaps the conscious purpose, of the universe". Scientific knowledge itself is held to be a minimum "ideal"; in any case, the real is known through the ideal.[52] In a more recent study he defends the "objectivity" of ideals on the ground that they appeal to "universal reason", and that all value-claims, including claims of knowledge as "a" value, must by nature be judged in terms of some objective ideal standard. And an objective reference is an "inherent element" in all true ideals, whether they be aesthetic or moral, in that they indicate "an attitude toward every possible object of will in other persons and in nature . . . an aspiration to transform the given subjective experience into something more meaningful and better grounded in the objective structure of the world".[53] Indeed, the objectivity of values is seen by him to be derived from the objectivity of ideals as necessary principles of interpretation; values "embody something universal" in that, if they be true values, they are verified by "objective" ideals. And the key-ideal is the ideal of "coherence": "When a value can take its place in a coherent system, then we treat it as a true value".[54] Furthermore, "if ideals are not objective—and, indeed, the basis of all objectivity, then there is no meaning to objectivity at all".[55] To speak of "objectivity" in this manner is possible, of course, only if one, as an idealistic empiricist, follows Hegel in identifying the "rational" (coherent) with the real.

The analysis of true ideals points to a "system of purposes in the universe beyond man . . . what spiritual thinkers have called the mind of God."[56] The religious ideal is the organization of all life with reference to faith in this divine realm, "an assertion that the highest ideal is real in some sense, in spite of the fact that the ideal is not and cannot be fully realized in mind and nature as we experience them".[57] Religious values are experienced "when man takes an attitude toward value-experience as a whole and toward its dependence on powers beyond man".[58] They are characterized by a unique sense of dependence upon the ground of the universe as distinguished from any particular environmental conditions; by the mystical tone of worship and prayer; and by a consciousness of divine aid and of submission to cosmic purposes.[59] Such experiences can be meaningful, Brightman claims, only if they have truly objective reference; that is, only if God exists. All vital experiences of religious value claim objectivity, and the analysis of the total system of values and ideals verifies this claim. If value were only subjective desire it could easily be fulfilled, and the eternal tension and conflict stemming from the compelling sense of obligation would be resolved. There must, therefore, be some normative objective reference to account for these inescapable facts of value-experience. Furthermore, since all reality must be related to consciousness, and since the character of obligation is essentially living and personal, it can only follow that the supreme ideals demand as their systematic "ground" a conscious and purposeful Supreme Person. This does not mean that supreme values are already "realized" in the perfection of this supreme consciousness, as we shall see, but only that the "perfectibility" of the universe is objectively rooted in reality.[60] One is driven to realize the compelling objectivity of the divine through the "dialectic of desire", in which reason leads one from the desire for pleasure through various ideal stages to the "desire for the Supreme Person" and a consequent dissatisfaction with all partial value-achievements.[61]

We have indicated in some detail the nature of Brightman's appeal to value experience in establishing the case for theistic belief because it represents a major strain in his thought and illustrates the scope of his conception of empirical method as involving the "transcendental" and his conception of "objectivity" as rationality. Surely it is confusing to term this speculative type of deduction from empirically given value-experiences itself "empirical"! It also indicates his attempt to harmonize the influences of Ritschl and Schleiermacher in empirical theology, whereas others would distinguish between "valuational" and "empirical" elements.[62]

In addition to the argument from value-experience, Brightman has also more recently stressed the significance of the broader facts of natural teleology as such. The very rationality of the universe suggests, he thinks, that there must be a unitary and rational "ground". More especially do the teleological "facts" of the natural world suggest cosmic purpose. The purposive functions of organisms pointed out by Drietsch and others; the significance of the "arrival of the fit" in the "survival of the fittest"; the human experiences of purpose in "spiritual life"; the complex interactions of mind and body and the general mystery of natural law, which remains a mystery after all the descriptive operations of science—all of these "facts of experience" suggest a conscious purpose at the heart of things, he feels. The emergence of novelty in the world and the broad facts of "emergent evolution" can be accounted for only in terms of active purposeful Divine Mind, he believes. But more especially does the very nature of personality itself demand an account of "extra-personal" reality in terms of the conscious will of a Supreme Person. Nothing "lower" than personality could account for the emergence and existence of persons.[63] All of these facts, he thinks, point to the reasonableness of theistic belief. Such belief is, of course, not completely coherent because it involves the meaning of the whole universe—all of the facts of unfinished experience—and such an insight is not likely to be attained by finite beings. But it is not incoherent, and it does justice to a wider range of experience than any competing hypothesis. Thus a truly empirical approach to the problems of existence and value lead most reasonably to belief in God.

It may be wise, before evaluating in more detail this approach to theism, to indicate briefly the "empirical" view of God which Brightman finds emerging from his analysis. Since all the actual data "empirically available" are conscious experiences, and the God inferred therefrom must be consistent with this fact and explanatory of it; since all physical forces are known only in consciousness and seem to display the purposive direction of conscious will; since value-experience points to a personal ground of obligation; and since religious experience bears witness to a personally responsive divine reality; therefore we must think of God as a spiritual personality.[64] This divine personality may be thought of as bearing all the marks of human personality mentioned above, with the additional characteristics of being "uncreated and eternal". He must also be conceived as eternally struggling with an uncreated and eternal "Given" (see below), as one having no material body but whose body is "a form of his conscious experience with which we may interact"; as having some types of experience unknown to men; as being the creator of all other persons, who are both dependent upon, yet distinct, from him; and as alone being "completely personal", with no break in conscious purposiveness.[65]

Morally God is the supremely valuable being, and goodness is his "most essential attribute".[66] As the supreme source of value he is one and not many because natural law is a unity and value appears in a world of natural law, and because value-experience itself points to a system of values constituting a whole in terms of which partial realizations are to be judged (see above).[67]

But more recently Brightman has held that a "truly empirical" analysis of values and purpose in experience and nature leads to the conclusion that the supremely good Person must be finite in power, evolving and struggling with a "Given" element in his own being. The facts of evolution reveal dysteleologies, meaningless processes, "bad guesses", and the existence of purely destructive beings in the world. And there are certain stark tragedies of human moral experience which cannot be "explained away" if God be viewed as both perfectly good and omnipotent.[68] Furthermore, reality itself seems to consist experientially of action, form, and content, and the hypothesis which accounts for reality must embody these elements.[69] Again, the nature of the Hegelian dialectic, the empirical method of consciousness, reveals an element of struggle at the heart of the process of synthetic progress, though Hegel failed to take this insight seriously enough. Then, too, the fact of human freedom, a presupposition of moral experience itself, can only mean that God is in some respects "finite" with respect to knowledge, at least with respect to knowledge of the future. This fact coupled with the compelling facts of evolutionary theory, can only mean that God is genuinely temporal. History, if taken seriously, can only reveal a God who acts in history and is thus temporal; the idea of progress demands such a concept, as does the reality of struggle and development in moral life. All of this means that God is "eternal" only in the sense that he endures as an active agent through all time. "The God of religion, from everlasting to everlasting, is a temporal being . . . not a timeless being . . . an ever enduring creator. His existence is an eternally changing present".[70] Creation is a "growing process in time", unbegun and unending; God's "eternity" is simply his expanded "specious present", in which he knows all the past and anticipates all the future, though not knowing the specific choices of his free creatures but knowing the consequences of choices if made. Thus he can, as James said, "always make the winning move", and is never overcome by evil. On the other hand, evil is never obliterated.[71]

Such a conception of a finite God is demanded, not only by the facts of value-experience, evolution, and the nature of consciousness itself, but it is also reflected in religious experience as such, thinks Brightman. "It seems to be the voice of religion that there is something above and beyond reason in the reasonable God".[72] Religious experience has always exalted God's dignity and value while at the same time satisfying man's need for comfort in misery and redemption from sin, and philosophical absolutism has too often emphasized the former insight to the exclusion of the latter. Religious experience has stressed the significance of the struggle between "light and darkness", "God and Satan", "Yin and Yang". And the German mystics, among others, have stressed the significance of the "darker" and "irrational" side of the Christian God. Religion has always demanded a power able to save men from all specific evils, but not from evil as such or from the disciplinary power of suffering which follows from freedom. Thus "we may go so far as to maintain the thesis that religious experience would be possible and necessary only if God were finite."[73]

In criticizing the views of men like Hocking with respect to evil, Brightman says that absolutism's appeal to ignorance when confronted by "surd" evil, should logically involve scepticism with reference to apparent goods. When one ascribes these evils to the divine will or holds that, in the light of eternity or from the perspective of "the whole" they are really good, he does not "explain" them but really makes good and evil ultimately indistinguishable. This dilemma is avoided if one holds that they are the results of the "Given" in the Person of God himself. Furthermore, when absolutists insist upon a realized perfection in the Absolute they cut the nerve of moral effort, as James correctly saw. But "the root of all objections to theistic absolutism" is, in brief, "its *unempirical character*". And "the case for belief in a finite God may be summed up by saying that it is empirically adequate".[74]

The total conception of God which results from the "truly empirical" view is summarized as follows:

> God is a conscious person of perfect good will. He is the source of all value and so is worthy of worship and devotion. He is the creator of all other persons and gives them the power of free choice. Therefore his purpose controls the outcome of the universe. His purpose and his nature must be inferred from the way in which experience reveals them, namely, as being attained through effort, difficulty, and suffering. Hence there is in God's very nature something which makes the effort and pain of life necessary. There is within him . . . a passive element which enters into every one of his conscious states; as sensation, instinct, and impulse enter into ours, and constitutes a problem for him. This element we call the Given. The evils of life and the delays in the attainment of value, in so far as they come from God and not from human freedom, are thus due to his nature, yet not wholly due to his deliberate choice. His

will and his reason acting on the Given produce the world and achieve value in it.[75]

And this concept, according to Brightman, is found in at least some streams of Christian thought: in Gnosticism, in the trinitarian conception of the Atonement, and in the Arminian and Socinian emphases upon human freedom, suffering, and need. Indeed, "the resurrection of Jesus is the promise that the Cross is not God's last word to man . . . that God somehow finds suffering and death necessary to his ends . . . that no obstacles can block the advance of divine purpose".[76] Thus Brightman holds that his empirical concept of God is specifically Christian.

As for the question whether this theistic hypothesis involves "naturalism" or "supernaturalism", a question of particular interest to some of the other empirical philosophers of religion, Brightman maintains that it is really "inclusive naturalism".[77] If what is meant by naturalism is primarily methodological in import, taking the insights of the natural sciences as normative, rather than a metaphysical doctrine like materialism, then, he says, one needs only to add "interpretation" to arrive at a view such as his own. Methodological naturalism "is very close to the method adopted (by him), and is the only tenable alternative to rationalistic apriorism or a supernatural revelationism".[78]

Various criticisms have been offered of this type of theism, and specifically of the concept of God which emerges as its end-product.[79] It has been suggested that God cannot be both *the* supreme value, the *system* of absolute ideals, and the creator of all values, at once; again, that when Brightman admits the relevance of "timeless" essences and subsistences, it is difficult to account for these in terms of a temporal God; and, more particularly, that the idea of the finite God does not "explain" those facts of experience which Brightman points to as demanding such a conception, but really restates the problems raised. The doctrine of the "Given", it has been pointed out, rests upon a failure to distinguish between externality and otherness; in making the cosmic process immanent *in* God, there can be nothing external to him, and hence all facts must somehow be taken into the total God-idea. Too, the "Given" as lately described by him seems to be the source of much value as well as of disvalue, in that "laws of reason" and "sense-qualities" are accounted for thereby. Rather than account for evil, it is claimed, the "Given" is little more than an *asylum ignorantia*.[80] Brightman, it is pointed out, can avoid "the obvious speculative objections to Manichaeism only by reintroducing dualism into God"! And, if the source of evil lies in God's nature, how can he be called "infinitely good"? Again, is it actually true that the history of religious experience bears witness to the need of such a concept, especially the experience of Mohammedanism, Judaism, and Christianity, with their emphasis upon the transcendence and omnipotence of God? Brightman admits that God must have some attributes and experiences which transcend human understanding, but his statement that a truly transcendent God is "utterly unrelated to what is revealed in experience" holds "only if we rule out of court a rendition *ex parte Dei* of what admittedly excludes the grasp of human understanding". Indeed, one writer has gone so far as to say that he

> never faces—and surely it should be faced in a work on the philosophy of religion—the Christian claim that its divinely revealed doctrines of creation and redemption offer to men's imperfect comprehension a more *reasonable* solution to the problem of evil than any other alternative, and one that is at the same time in harmony with living religious experience.[81]

It is not our purpose here to discuss such criticisms at length; Brightman has sought to deal with most of them himself.[82] It does indeed seem that there are a number of difficulties in his view from the standpoint of living religion, particularly Christianity. It is questionable, for instance, whether the meaning of the Resurrection in Christian symbolism is, as he claims, that the Cross, and the struggling, suffering God pictured thereby, constitutes a victorious "word" in itself, or whether Christian symbolism suggest the paradoxical idea of "eternal" triumph *in* and *over* time by one who "*has* overcome the world". Does the "eternal" nature of God actually mean, in Christian terminology, simply that God endures through all time or, indeed, "develops" in the progressive experience of creation? Is there not something rather of the *transtemporal* or *supra-temporal* (not, to be sure, the *a*-temporality or time*lessness* of subsistences) and not simply the *pan*temporal in such symbols as that of "the great I-Am", and more specifically, in the Judeo-Christian eschatological idea? Again, while it is true that Christian doctrine has not attempted to "explain away" the fact of evil, it has asserted, whether "rationally" or not, that The Eternal "entered history" at a point *in time* and "overcame" evil thereby. It may be that Brightman's attempt to face the facts of change and dysteleology more squarely than absolutism has done, but at the same time to claim both a Christian reference and to make the interpretation "reasonable" by identifying "eternity" with pantemporality and making the triumph of God a continuous, hence also eternally, unfinished process, illustrates rather sharply the difficulties involved in translating living religious symbols, with their peculiarly "personal and ultimate" reference, into the more literal language of philosophy and science.

However, our chief interest here is in the claim of Brightman that his account of God is alone "truly empirical" and is a definitive illustration of the most fruitful employment of empirical method in philosophy of religion. The claim that the idea of God as personal is empirical rests, in part, upon his analysis of experience, as such, with the resultant belief that all reality is of necessity "in, of or for persons". We have suggested above certain difficulties with this view; we may add here a further suggestion that a peculiar difficulty arises when one attempts to expand the concept of "person" to embrace a being or reality possessing the other characteristics which Brightman ascribes to God. Other problems emerge with reference to the relation of the "Supreme Person" to his creatures. Professor Wieman, as we shall see, offers several cogent objections to the empirical validity of this idea. Again, the concept of God as supremely valuable, and the case for his "objective" status as *the* supreme value, rests in part if not wholly upon what would seem to be the rationalistic thesis that "the rational is the real" in value-analysis. Is it true that an experimental approach to value-experience demands any notion of *a* supreme value or *a* source of all values? If any such "being", the ground of all experience, discoverable *in* experience?

It would seem, rather, that the positing of any such transcendent ground or goal follows from the rationalistic ideal of a "finished" view of "unfinished" experience, for an overall view of "the whole". Yet Brightman is critical of traditional transcendentalism and, in his attempt to face squarely the facts of temporality and particularity in value-experience, he is driven to modify his idea of the Absolute through the introduction of the notion of the "given". One result of his empiricism is thus an abandonment of certain of the traditional emphases of ethical transcendentalism, while he at the same time retains a belief in a cosmic ground or Person which (or Who) is not "given" in the experience which it is to "explain", but is arrived at through a process of speculative deduction, and which embodies certain characteristics lying beyond the possibilities of human experience. It would seem that he loses thereby many of the values which may be associated with transcendentalism while at the same time falling short of a thoroughgoing empiricism.

For it is difficult to see just what sort of "explanation" of experience is afforded by an appeal to an empirical Absolute. If one is not to go "beyond the facts" of unfinished experience in attributing characteristics to such an Absolute, then one's understanding of experience is hardly enriched by the entertainment of such a concept. As Hume pointed out, any hypothesis about a "ground" of existence can at best affirm, on strictly empirical grounds, that such a "ground" is the basis for just those facts which are known apart from its employment. What, then, is added to empirical knowledge?[83] As we shall see, other philosophers who have sought to be more precisely empirical in their analysis of value-experience have come to adopt dualistic or pluralistic views. Indeed, it would seem that a thoroughgoing dualism is logically demanded by the facts which Brightman marshals in support of his concept of the "finite God", if it be granted that some overall "explanation" of goods and evils is empirically demanded. The dualistic idealism of J. E. Boodin, to which we presently turn, would seem to be more consistent in this respect. But Brightman, apparently because of lingering elements of monistic absolutism in his philosophy, finds that it is more "coherent" to include the incoherent within the experience of the Cosmic Person.

The result, we believe, epitomizes his general conception of empirical method. Abandoning certain presuppositions of traditional rationalism, he seeks to take seriously the significance of time and contingency in particular and unfinished experience and would embody at least some of the emphases of experimentalism in his methodology. He no longer believes that "eternal" and "certain" truths can be arrived at a priori, that is "apart from consciousness", at least in most realms of knowledge, but that all generalizations about experience must be based upon observation and expressed in propositions which can be only hypothetically true. Thus his defense of the theistic hypothesis is made in terms of an appeal to certain facts of the natural world, as interpreted in a certain manner, and to certain facts of human experience, with an emphasis upon the significance of moral and religious experience. In this connection he would take seriously the presence of dysteleology in nature and "surd evil" in human experience.

However, his view of experience is, we believe, exaggeratedly subjectivistic, and many of his metaphysical conclusions are based in part upon what seems to be an unempirical interpretation of experience in general, and of the knowledge-situation in particular. Similarly, his view of empirical method as appealing to "coherence" in the interpretation of the "whole" of experience for its norm seems to embody certain goals and emphases more appropriate to rationalistic absolutism. These are reflected most clearly in his analysis of value-experience and his defense of the "objectivity" of ideals as revealing the "objective" structure of reality, and in his appeal to an immanent but absolute "ground" of value and nature in order to "explain" the facts of experience. In claiming to know the essential character of this Absolute and thus of the general direction of all experience, he falls short of that open and tentative experimentalism and pluralism which characterize a "tough-minded" empirical temper and method. And the Absolute, when rendered strictly accountable to heteroge-

neous and ongoing experience, emerges as a bifurcated, if not disinte-
grated, Absolute, the hybrid product of a hybrid method. We shall find in
Boodin's idealism an attempt to avoid some of these difficulties.

III: J. E. Boodin, *Empirical Realist and Cosmic Idealist*

The philosophy of John Elof Boodin (1869–) offers a third illustration
of the competing influences of Royce and James in contemporary American idealism. In his suggestive and original position, Boodin seeks to avoid
many of the positions held by other idealists which seem incompatible with
a genuinely empirical approach. He claims no single type of experience as
normative in defending his cosmic idealism, does not place an exaggerated
emphasis upon the subjective in his analysis of experience, and evolves a
pluralistic metaphysic and dualistic cosmology through what he takes to
be a consistent application of experimental method. At the same time he
finds a form of cosmic idealism suggested by his contextualistic account of
reality, and in the articulation of his views he employs religious symbols
which he believes are essentially Christian. It therefore seems appropriate
to conclude our chapter on idealistic religious empiricism with a brief
exposition and examination of his system.

Boodin's intellectual background and development are similar in many
respects to those of Hocking and Brightman. Emigrating to this country
in 1887 from Sweden, he engaged in various occupations, including some
forms of manual labor, before beginning an academic career. These experiences, he says, stimulated an empirically realistic view of life and an
appreciation of the richly complex character of human nature. His philosophical interest, following upon and developing within an early religious
piety, was first stimulated by James, whom he read with critical avidity.
After undergraduate work at Brown he went to Harvard to study with
James and Royce, as well as with Everett, Palmer, and Münsterberg.
There, he writes, Royce was his "master". But in his doctoral dissertation
he developed an original criticism of the absolutist view of time, for which
James afforded sympathetic encouragement. Then he broadened the scope
of his criticism and finally, during the early debate centering around the
pragmatic school, he offered an essay designed to "clarify the issues" which
was approved by James as a clear interpretation of what pragmatism
should be. Dewey has subsequently incorporated many of the restrictions
which he then suggested, he says. His view of time was finally developed,

after considerable stimulation from Alexander's *Space, Time, and Deity*, into an interpretation of cosmic evolution which defends a Platonic doctrine of interactionism against that of emergence. A critical reaction to early forms of pragmatism has also led him to emphasize structure as well as function in his views of truth and reality, and he has also been "obliged on further thought to recognize the pragmatic reality of the world of ideal values". The latter insight was expressed in his volume, *Truth and Reality*,[1] while the reality of form and structure in a world of flux was defended in *A Realistic Universe*.[2] In *Cosmic Evolution*[3] he put forward the hypothesis that measure and order in natural processes can best be accounted for in terms of spiritual control, and this view was developed into a natural theology, in *God and Creation*.[4]

In his analysis of the knowledge-situation Boodin seeks to avoid the subjectivism of psychologistic idealists. The problem of "taking the same object twice" in one experience-history and of several individuals' "taking the same object" is solved by him in terms of three cognitive contexts, physical, social, and individual, rather than in terms of "Other Mind" or Cosmic Person. Objective continuity is often explicable in terms of the first context alone, though it is actually realized only in the third. While the three contexts are interrelated, each has definite characteristics of its own, and analysis of the knowledge-situation does not necessarily issue in an appeal to any sort of absolute context or "whole".[5] Whereas naïve and critical realists both err in supposing that substances and qualities may "exist" independently of a "field", a "functional realist" would hold that "bifurcation of thing and environment is vicious, that things exist only in fields, in mutuality with other things, and that they have properties only in their dynamic relations". All activity is perspective; the activities of "nature" simply constitute the "primary perspective", while judgments about nature constitute "secondary perspectives". These two perspectives may vary independently of each other in physical and psychical histories, but they are not ultimately separated in our total "life in nature".

Conceptual elements are involved in all perceptions, and material "things" are not more directly "given" than are "spiritual" realities. The designation of certain experiential constants as "primary qualities" is based upon certain functional requirements alone and need not indicate any sort of primacy in "reality". On the contrary, immediate experience is qualitative as well as quantitative, and analyses which stress the ontological primacy of either aspect are based upon a misinterpretation of what are essentially functional abstractions. There is no "intuition" of either primary or secondary qualities, nor is the percipient organism of more significance in the perception of either class. Attention and awareness, the "introspection" which psychologistic idealists often stress, are to be understood as types of activity among others which must be considered in any adequate view of experience as a whole; this means that experience includes physical, organic, and psychical contexts or perspectives in close interrelation. And the objects of knowledge are dependent upon cognitive moments only for their cognitive significance, not for their "existence". Such objects may, in turn, be physical, organic, or psychical in character, "any aspect selected as datum by cognitive interest".[6]

Thus Boodin would avoid those distortions in the interpretation of experience which have characterized the analyses of other idealists. Such distortions have been reflected in other views of the method by which experience is to be investigated as well, and Boodin's more liberal account is likewise reflected in his interpretation of empirical method. In his early accounts of methodology he acknowledges indebtedness to James, saying that "we must judge the nature of reality by the consequences to the realizations of human purposes, instead of by *a priori* assumptions".[7] Classical empiricism he takes to be "only a half-way house" in that understanding of truth which is compatible with the modern employment of scientific method. Any adequate view of truth, he says, must combine the traditional emphasis upon "immediate luminosity" with a recognition of tentativeness and openness to further processes of verification. Truth, however, does not *consist* in such verifications, else it could never "exist". Rather "positive truth-value" follows from "the felt consistency or fluent termination in its intended object" of cognitive experience. Experience "becomes truth" only through conceptual construction motivated by purposive volitional attitudes, and percepts are to be interpreted as termini of such constructions, as "verification-stuff". But only meanings are thus "created", not the objects meant. Thus Boodin seeks to do justice to the "feeling" of certainty stressed by Hocking and others while retaining at the same time the full force of experimental method as affording the criterion of truth. Other empiricists, of course, might claim that his continued emphasis upon "immediate luminosity" and "felt consistency" is unnecessary for, if not incompatible with, a thorough-going experimentalism.[8] However, Boodin stresses this less than the idea of functional consequence in his general view of truth.

Turning now to his treatment of the central problems of religious philosophy, we find that his general views of experience and method lead him to positions in this field which are somewhat different from those of the other idealists whom we have studied. In his treatment of religious experience he is aware of the great variety of forms which such experience may take. "The final and all-inclusive function of religion is communion with God", he writes, and

This presence takes different forms in our life in accordance with our experience and temperament. It may be the stern call to duty, the sublimity of the moral law in our soul, more awesome than the starry heavens above. It may be the infinite friendliness of a life that envelopes us even as an atmosphere. It may be a vision into the deeper meaning of life with its infinite reaches. But always it means the sense of companionship and cooperation with God.[9]

Every true religious experience is a new creative synthesis. God does not repeat Himself in human relations any more than in sunsets or the play of shadows on the mountains. The external setting is the body of the occasion and cannot be divorced from the inner grace.[10]

At the same time he insists upon the essentially personal and poetic character of such experience; indeed, he speaks of religion as "the poetry of life", and his own religious writings are frequently lyrical in quality. Over-intellectualized accounts of religious experience and philosophical doctrines of God which seek to defend theism in terms of modern knowledge are "bought with a price", he feels.

The tendency has been to lose the sense of the intimate presence of the divine, vitally affecting every function of everyday life, and to substitute, for the personal relation which simpler souls have felt, an abstract God who is aloof from our individual concerns. . . . We have intellectualized the spiritual relation instead of making it first of all feeling and conduct.[11]

However, while religious experience may take many forms there is a certain unique and indefinable quality associated with such experience which distinguishes it from other types. There is "an immediate experience of the quality of the divine . . . an experience of community with a reality that has a spiritual quality . . . more than a community with matter, more than a community with living organisms or . . . finite minds." But it is impossible to define such experience completely in terms of other kinds. "All definitions of religious experience are circular. They presuppose the very essence which they attempt to define". Religious experience is not simply that of "morality touched with emotion", unless the "emotion" be distinctively religious. It is not simply a sense of "dependence upon a higher power", unless the higher power is seen to be divine in quality. Nor is it simply mystical absorption, unless it be absorption in the divine; similarly, it cannot be described simply in terms of "awe" or value-experience. "Our rationalization of the religious experience must not be confused with the experience itself. . . . The reality of the divine requires no proof. . . . Nothing of importance can be proved."[12] We may ask, however, whether the experience of the divine throws any light upon the world of which we are a part and upon the significance of our life in it, whether it adds a new and desirable quality to life. And religious experience when most dynamic has colored and ordered other types of experience into general patterns of the "whole of life". Art, knowledge, and morality have all drawn from the sense of the supernatural a dynamic motive and integration.[13] Religious experience, in brief, has led to "creative spirit—the striving for wholeness . . . the feeling for the whole".[14]

Now this view seems to be similar, in some respects, to that of Hocking and Brightman. Like Hocking, Boodin insists upon the significance of a "feeling for the whole", but like Brightman he refuses to set up any one kind of expression of such experience as normative. However, he differs from both in ascribing to such experience a uniquely and indefinably religious status rather than describing it in terms of a general analysis of the knowledge-situation or defending its validity in terms of general metaphysical presuppositions. He is aware of its imaginative and poetic character, and in judging its significance he would point primarily to its results or conduct. However, we may ask whether it is fruitful, in the light of his analysis, to speak of "religious experience" as a specific type. It seems rather that what Boodin is suggesting is that there is a certain quality of experience appearing under certain conditions as an element within or a dimension of various types of experience, which may be called a religious quality. Though this question may be largely one of definition, it is related, as we shall see, to his general view of the religious referent as described in metaphysical terms and thus may be of some importance. Insofar as various types of experience may or may not be religious in import, depending upon the "experience and temperament" of the experient and the general cultural context in which he finds himself, is it not misleading to use the broader term "religious experience" as if it referred to a specific type to be compared or contrasted with moral, esthetic, and other types?

In any event, Boodin does seek to rest his case for the validity of religious ideals upon their functional significance for life. In a lecture delivered at Harvard in 1899, before the pragmatic approach to religion had gained general recognition, he declared that religious believers are led by *practical* considerations to add to the inorganic, organic, and psychical contexts

an ultimate spiritual environment which shall be the objectivity and fulfillment of our fragmentary human ideals. . . . The same criterion may be applied to [this] as has been applied to other kinds of environment. I can see no difference as regards the test of religious concepts or hypotheses from the test of the scientific . . . in any case the idea must be proved by its consequences.[15]

And, among the most important consequences of a religious ideal are the social, "for it is the function of religion to interpret and idealize social relations. . . . The real religion of a people [is] the matrix of customs and ideals which actually controls men's conduct and for which they are willing to fight and die".[16] While it is true that religion is in part "an affair of the intellect", it is also true that "true thought is rooted in social relations. . . . Religion is more than thought. . . . It is a social bond, a spiritual compound". And what is needed today is a new sense of the sacramental character of social relations, a recovery of the meaning of "sacraments sanctifying real human relations and stimulating what is best in us. . . . All human activities should be made sacramental as indeed they were in earlier religions".[17] Since religious ideals make for social cohesiveness, heighten morality, and lead to "the highest development of life", they seem to be functionally verified in this area.

Of course one is faced with the question as to *which* religious ideals are valid on this score, and Boodin seeks to prove that the basic ideal of love as taught by Jesus has, in the course of human experience, proved itself normative. Christianity, he says, is "the highest religion to us because it, as no other, furnishes, in the simplest and completest way, that environment of the soul which satisfies and makes objective its highest yearning for the highest good".[18] Similarly, in the Preface to his most recent book he writes: "If the reader should feel after reading this book that what I call the Religion of Tomorrow is only a new statement of the religion of Jesus of Nazareth, I shall feel happy, but I shall maintain that it is the religion of the future".[19]

Now various questions may be raised with reference to this type of "verification" of a specific religious ideal. It may be asked, for instance, whether there is not a certain circularity in claiming the validity of one ideal because it makes for the "highest development of life" and then describing the latter in terms of the ideal to be verified. The same type of question may be raised concerning the meaning of such terms as "real human relations" and "what is best in us" and the criteria by which these are to be defined. A procedure of the sort suggested by Boodin seems to involve certain assumptions which it would perhaps be better to make explicit. Otherwise, statements of faith or belief may be confused with assertions of knowledge. And, insofar as Boodin claims an essentially Christian basis for the religious ideals which he believes to be valid, we must inquire whether other features of his religious philosophy may be said to be compatible with the main stream of Christian tradition.

For a more complete view of what he takes "the meaning of God in human experience" to be, it is necessary to relate the concept more specifically to his general view of metaphysics and cosmology. In the former the contextual principle suggested above plays a dominant rôle. There is, he believes, no dominant class of being, though "energy" may conveniently be described as the broadest neutral activity-concept. Materialism and some forms of idealism have erroneously based their cases on the thesis that only like can produce like; idealism has assumed that "thinking", a new fact in the emergent series of reality, must somehow be traced back to the beginning, and that the unity of understanding must be hypostatized in existence. A functional and contextual approach to the problems views this type of reasoning as fallacious. Experience is not a mental substance; it is a relation. While idealists are right in holding that mind is a unique element in reality and not a product of matter, and that nature appears to be mind-controlled, they err in assuming that therefore the whole of reality must be mental. Mind is a unique pattern of existence in itself, but "the world in which we live is a pluralistic world with various histories and their interactions. We have no right to suppose that the special characteristics of certain parts hold for the aggregate".[20] It may be fruitful to conceive of reality in terms of three energy-systems including the mechanical, involving mass; the electrical, involving light and magnetism; and the "conative", involving mind.

However, just as religious experience refers to an entity which seems to give added meaning to other kinds of experience, so metaphysical analysis suggests that the pluralistic contexts of reality must somehow be interrelated and controlled by one over-all context or "field". This field may be described as "spiritual", and

like the "circumnambient air", pervading all the worlds, in the large and in the small, overlapping all other fields, measuring the unit and constituting the structure, the soul of the whole. As we conceive material events as measured and guided by a cosmic field, so we must conceive all events of history as measured and guided by a spiritual field so far as their inertia permits. . . . God is the spiritual field in which everything lives and moves and has its being . . . the soul of the whole, suffusing it with meaning.

As such he is best understood in terms of "cosmic mind", that which gives form to chaos, as in the Platonic vision. Then "cosmic space becomes the field of the infinite expansiveness of God and the rhythm of cosmic time becomes the reflex of the rhythm of his eternal activity". And to advance in the scale of life is "to become more attuned to the divine field", while that which resists degenerates until it becomes "mere raw material to be recreated from the beginning". The world is thus the "body" of God, not as the physical body is the body of the human soul, but as "sound is the

body of music or instrumentation gives body to harmony". Spirit is inde
pendent of matter, but without spirit matter would be chaos.[21]

Thus matter is looked upon, in Platonic fashion, as material for organi
zation, while form ("spirit" or God) is the eternal, creative, dynami
structure. Form and matter are, to use Augustine's phrase, "concreated'
Their properties are, respectively, inertia-spontaneity, entropy-creativit
and so on. Such a dualism, Boodin says, makes mechanism meaningful i
a given context, while it at the same time makes spirit meaningful as pur
mechanism could not. Furthermore, it accounts for the scale of forms an
prospective adaptation, for the intelligibility and aesthetic grandeur o
the world, and for the reality of struggle and tragedy as spiritual monisr
could not.[22] This latter claim is of special interest for our study, in th
light of Brightman's defense of a limited God, or what we have called
"bifurcated absolute", as empirically demanded by the nature of evil an
of time.

In his cosmology Boodin criticizes all forms of "preformationism", i
which he includes, in the Western tradition, the views of the Stoics, Lei
niz, Kant, Schelling, Hegel, Nietzsche, Schopenhauer, and Whitehead, a
"failing to take time seriously" and ultimately eliminating true novelt
and contingency. Though structure is real, so is a measure of indeterm
nacy, and history has many possible outcomes. "The world in which we li
is . . . highly venturesome, thrilling and dangerous . . . in which w
must create our own rôles".[23] Theories of "emergence", on the other hand
are in the last analysis, merely descriptive. And the traditional Christia
doctrine of "monistic creationism", he feels, simply removes the proble
from the realm of reasonable investigation by scientific means and "puts
in the realm of magic". It leads logically to predestination and the loss
all initiative, and also renders the problem of evil inscrutable, or el
makes God responsible for evil, which for "an ethical spirit" is blasphem
Indeed Boodin asks whether it is

> possible to be sure that what we eulogistically conceive as omnipoten
> and omniscience have any meaning as applied to God? They are rhetor
> as far as we are concerned. But that there is a power working for trut
> righteousness, and beauty . . . is the great inspiration of all who wo
> for the realization of ideals in a struggling, pluralistic world.[24]

It is better rather to view creation as an eternal process of struggle b
tween matter and spirit. This view is itself to be found in at least son
phases of the Judeo-Christian tradition, Boodin says, citing Genesis wi
its account of the ordering of the "void", and the writings of Clement
cases in point. And the dualism is ethical as well as cosmological: the go
and the beautiful "order" the evil and the ugly, and right is in conflict wi

wrong.[25] The pain of birth and struggle are real, and the world is best understood as the stage of an eternal drama of redemption, in which spirit works with infinite patience to save from chaos and destruction all types of recalcitrant "matter". The great cosmic tragedy lies in the fact that "few are chosen". "All is not well with the world, but at least it offers the opportunity of grand heroism, of sublime loyalty; and in such high moments spirit confronts the world." Matter is destructible but spirit is eternal, and we have occasional "intuitions" of its eternal victory, leading to a reasonable hope that, through suffering, spirit may save spirit in a cooperative venture of salvation.[26] In any event, we cannot think of God as the creator of evil. In practice Christianity has avoided doing so through its doctrine of the Fall. But if God be limited, it is from "without" and not from "within": "there is no limitation in God, since God's life is perfect in its own right. The limitation lies in the finite response to God . . . there is no evidence for this universe being a perfect whole though there is evidence of a whole-control".[27]

With this fuller exposition of Boodin's metaphysical concept of God before us, let us return to the question raised by his analysis of religious experience: to what extent is his view consistently empirical, if to be empirical means to employ experimental method as he conceives the latter? By refusing to restrict the experiential basis of the God-concept to any specific expression of religious experience, he avoids the problems which are raised by this type of procedure and in this respect he is close to Brightman. On the other hand, he is not restricted in his view of the empirical subject-matter in general, as Brightman apparently is, and he does not rest his case for cosmic idealism upon any form of the subjectivist fallacy; nor does he claim special "transcendental" reference for value-experience as affording a unique basis for belief in an "objective" source of value. In his earlier essay on the validity of religious ideals he approached this type of claim, but subordinated it to the general functional efficacy of the God-idea. Furthermore, he seeks to avoid any form of absolutism or "eternalism" and takes a "radically realistic" view of time and of evil, which leads him to a cosmic dualism. In all these respects he may be said to be more consistent in the application of experimental method than either of the other two idealists, though not all of his cosmological ideas need be taken as inevitable consequences of *any* employment of this method. With reference to the "problem of evil", for instance, we suggested in the previous section that some empiricists would hold that the problem itself is a false one and that a pluralism not a dualism is adequate to account for those features of experience which are said to give rise to the issue.

Yet there are one or two points at which he seems to equivocate. We have said that he takes a radically realistic view of time and evil; yet in one pas-

sage he speaks of the perfect attributes of divinity as "future" in their
realization "only from our perspective" but wholly realized in the divine
nature itself.[28] To speculate about realities apart from their functional
relevance to "our perspective" is surely to depart from the strictly empirical and contextual analysis upon which he elsewhere insists. And his
descriptions of God as the "whole" or "spirit of the whole", and of some
sort of "whole-control" of the cosmos seems radically to modify the clear-
cut dualism which is otherwise insisted upon. In some contexts the dualism
seems to be complete; the ethico-religious implications are even compared
by him with Zoroastrianism. Yet he is led to say that the difference between
the natural and the supernatural is simply the difference between the
"piece-meal point of view and the whole point of view".[29] But if God be
the "spirit of the whole" or is associated with the "whole point of view",
how can he at the same time be completely other than and in opposition to
the matter and evil which enter into the picture of the whole? In this connection, how can Boodin maintain that matter and spirit are "concreated"
and of equal significance, but yet that matter is dependent upon spirit
while spirit is at the same time somehow independent of matter? If God is
only spirit, then there might be a third "context" including matter-and-
spirit. On the other hand, if God himself is this over-all context, as Boodin
seems to hold in his metaphysic, then some concept like Brightman's
"finite" God would seem to be called for, in that God-as-whole includes
the warring elements God-as-spirit and matter-evil.

This leads to further questions about his view of God as "spiritual field"
or the context which overlaps all other contexts, activating and ordering
them, and affording a medium of intercotextual communication and
translation. Does not such a concept vitiate the pluralism which, he believes, is implied by a consistent employment of experimental method? Is
there not a lingering monism or absolutism involved in this idea? The
answer to these questions hinges upon the problem whether the "spiritual"
is to be thought of as one context among others, just as his analysis of religious experience raises the question whether such experience is related
to others as the others are to each other. Now it would seem that if the "spiritual" context is that in terms of which all the others are finally meaningful and is not to be identified, even by analogy, with any specific one but is
rather somehow implied by each, then its relation to all other contexts is
different in principle from any possible relation of the dependent contexts to each other. Is it fruitful, then, to speak of it, too, as "a" context? Or
to be more specific, is it necessary, on the grounds of experimental metho
alone, to appeal to such an over-all context in order to discover the meaning of the others? Why is it not at least theoretically possible to "explain
the other contexts in terms of *each other*? These questions suggest that

while Boodin has criticized other idealists for hypostatizing ideas of "the whole", "other mind", and so on, he himself may actually be hypostatizing certain assumptions involved in contextualistic analysis. Whereas he suggests that a consistent employment of experimental method might issue in a radical pluralism, his own philosophy embodies a quasi-monistic framework for an ethical and cosmological dualism. And the adoption of such a system by him seems to be the result, as least in part, of an attempt to satisfy certain religious demands. This, in turn, may suggest that there are certain limitations inherent in the experimental ideal for the articulation of some forms of religious experience.

In any event, it seems fair to say, with reference to Boodin's claim that his is an essentially Christian philosophy of religion (except, of course, with respect to the doctrine of creation) that, as one reviewer has put it, he seems rather to have evolved a "mythology of science" or a "theology for natural scientists" but "not a philosophy of religion, least of all the Christian religion".[30] The essentially impersonal character of his concept of God as "spirit" and his rejection of the traditional Christian doctrines of creation and redemption in favor of ethical and cosmological dualism perhaps follow from his empirical analysis, but they are hardly compatible with the more "naïve" and paradoxical symbols in which Christians have usually expressed their faith. In summary, we may say that Boodin's views of experience and of empirical method lead him to avoid many of the questionable conclusions drawn by other idealists from what seem to be faulty analyses of these problems, and that his ethical dualism seems to be more compatible with a strictly empirical approach than do the monistic or quasi-monistic views of Hocking and Brightman in this respect. However, we believe that his insistence upon the reality of a "cosmic context" or "soul of the whole" reflects a quasi-absolutistic ideal more usually associated with rationalism, and that he is guilty of some measure of "hypostatization" in this connection. This, in turn, may be viewed as the result of an attempt to translate into more literal philosophical terms certain religious ideas which he himself says are more appropriately expressed in poetic and symbolic language.

It may be appropriate now to summarize briefly some of the significant features of idealistic empiricism with reference to religious philosophy, as illustrated in the systems examined in this chapter. Each of the philosophers studied seeks to base his religious views upon what he takes to be a careful examination of the "facts of experience". Furthermore, each would recognize the presence within experience of certain affective, volitional, and "irrational" factors which rationalistic idealists have failed to take seriously, and each seeks to do justice to modern scientific accounts of the natural world in his total system. The significance of the concrete and the particular, the novel and the contingent, is recognized in some measure by all. And all would take account of the data afforded by various forms of religious experience in the working out of their religious philosophies.

Broader views of experience and an attempt to "take time serious" are reflected also in these idealists' methodologies. Hocking recognizes the hypothetical and tentative character of scientific inquiry and would incorporate these emphases, at least in part, within his own method. Brightman goes further and maintains that all truth is of necessity hypothetical and that only "practical" certainty is possible in any area, while Boodin would adopt a thoroughgoing experimentalism in his account of reality on a contextual basis. Thus the older rationalistic ideal of finished and certain truth which has characterized much absolute idealism is explicitly abandoned, at least to some extent, by our philosophers.

These basic positions find direct expression in their treatment of more specifically religious problems. Hocking would base his defense of theism upon the implications of natural and social experience and the assumptions which he believes are necessary for the free employment of scientific method as well as upon direct mystical experience of God. Similarly Brightman finds the existence of a Cosmic Person, which is suggested in religious experience, also rationally demanded as a presupposition of natural knowledge, as well as by the facts of value-experience and by the implications of modern scientific cosmology. And Boodin believes that a functional and contextual analysis of experience points to the existence of a Cosmic Spirit activating, ordering, and "redeeming" the world, with whom men may have communion in various forms of experience.

Furthermore, our idealists seek to face squarely the facts of evil and tragedy in their accounts of the nature of God and his relation to men. Hocking insists upon the temporal reality of evil and the necessity for free and earnest moral struggle, though he continues to posit the notion of an ultimate transmutation of evil from the perspective of God. Brightman, taking natural dysteleology, time, and "surd" evil more seriously, is forced to conclude that God Himself must be "finite" in power to overcome all evil in principle and that He is eternally warring against and overcoming specific elements of "the Given" within Himself. And Boodin believes that only a clear-cut ethical and cosmological dualism can do justice to the facts of cosmic evolution and moral conflict. Thus the views of our three philosophers afford suggestive illustrations of what may be termed successive stages in "empiricizing the Absolute". As a result of their empirical emphases the Absolute ceases to be a transcendent, timeless, and perfect unity and becomes an immanent, temporal "power for goodness", eternally strug gling against equally "real" forces of evil, "within" or "without". Or, to put it in religious terms, the empirical approach to God by our idealists results in the abandonment of the doctrine of the transcendence of God.

But we have raised various questions concerning the extent to which these thinkers are genuinely empirical if to be empirical means to take an inclusive and undistorted view of experience and to apply the experimental method of scientific inquiry in the interpretation of experience. And we have seen in the views of Hocking and Brightman an exaggerated emphasis upon the subjective in experience which is closely bound up with their metaphysics and methodology. With respect to method, we find that Hocking would supplement the free and open operation of scientific inquiry with some intuitive assurance of certainty and finished truth, while Brightman would incorporate in his understanding of "empirical method" various types of inquiry to such an extent that he seems guilty of "the fallacy of the suppressed correlative". Furthermore, we have questioned Hocking's appeal to one specific form of religious experience as normative and have maintained that a more truly empirical approach would take account of variety and the role of cultural context in this connection. We have also maintained that Brightman's appeal to value experience as demanding the "existence" of an objective source and judge of values is based upon the rationalistic notion that the rational is the real.

But it seems that the basic common emphasis of all the idealists is upon the significance of the idea of "the whole". All of them believe that it is possible to have empirical knowledge of the essential or definitive character of "the whole" of experience or reality, and that such knowledge is of primary importance in "explaining" or understanding the "parts". Hocking turns to the notion of Other Knower or Other Mind as affording the final locus of such explanation, while Brightman turns to a Cosmic Person and Boodin to a cosmic context or Spirit. Thus, while they recognize in some measure the significance of plurality in experience and the tentativeness and openness which a genuine recognition of its temporal quality demands, they seem at the same time to retain at least the rationalistic *ideal* of a "finished" view of reality. And when they attribute ultimate ontological status to such an ideal they seem to indulge in the same sort of "hypostatization" which has characterized absolutism in general. Indeed, we maintain that it is just this absolutism, even though it be expressed in terms of a divided and struggling Absolute, which compromises the "tough-mindedness" of our empirical idealists and results in their retention of certain views which would seem to be incompatible with an unambiguous and thoroughgoing empiricism. In the next chapter we shall see whether a realistic or a naturalistic approach may be more consistently empirical.

3

RELIGIOUS REALISM AND THEISTIC NATURALISM

I: D. C. Macintosh, *Common-Sense Realist*

Douglas Clyde Macintosh (1877–) has perhaps done more than any other philosopher of religion to popularize the term "empirical theology". It has been nearly a quarter of a century since he first published his well-known *Theology as an Empirical Science,*[1] and during subsequent years he has defended in many works the thesis that a critical analysis and interpretation of a certain type of religious experience may yield the data and laws of an empirically scientific theological system. Hocking, as we have seen, while seeking an empirical foundation for his objective idealism, makes no claim that theology as such may be scientifically established, and Brightman has modified his personalism only in the direction of empirical method of a kind. Macintosh has consistently criticized all forms of idealism as incompatible with what he takes to be the valid employment of empirical method and has insisted that a strictly empirical religious philosophy must rest upon a realistic theory of knowledge, both general and religious.

Since we shall wish to show in this Section that Macintosh's own religious and intellectual background and development play a decisive role in his understanding of empirical theology, we shall preface our exposition and evaluation of his thought with a rather full account of some of these influences. He was reared, he tells us, in an atmosphere of strict religious piety and reverence for Puritan morals. "The type of religious training with which as a child I was in immediate contact made me familiar at an early age with all the principal evangelical concepts. . . . Religion as we knew it was not only orthodox and evangelical but . . . evangelistic." At the age of ten he underwent a mild experience of "conversion" which he now holds to be of dubious value; but at fourteen there was a vivid experience of "assurance" at an evangelistic prayer-meeting, which was of crucial and lasting significance. "I felt that it was a momentous transaction. . . . I was enabled thereby to enter into *what long afterwards I came to speak as the right religious adjustment* . . . first, as presupposed, aspiration after a truly Christian life; then, concentration upon a Divine Being regarded as absolutely good and reliable; abandon of one's self and one's will to the holy will of the Divine Being; expectant waiting, and finally an act of faith deliberately accepting reconciliation with God and appropriating the moral reinforcement felt to be needed. . . ." Today, "with due respect to psychologists of religion and votaries of religious education", he is still convinced that the "conversion experience of my fourteenth year was quite normal and morally wholesome. . . . I firmly believe that no event of my life has been so fundamentally determinative in the Christian direction as that experience".[2]

Thus, in his recent volume on *Personal Religion,* he offers, as suggestive case-material for the development of a "modern evangelicalism", an account of the religious life of certain New England Puritans, with the suggestion that Christianity today must attempt to recapture certain features of this type of personal faith. To this end he offers a reinterpretation of many of the basic concepts of evangelical Christianity[3] and concludes that in the "general type of treatment to be recommended for the Church's present-day ills" should be included "a renewed and revitalized Christian evangelicalism" which will involve, "as a dynamic evangelicalism always has involved, the presentation of the Christian gospel of the saving grace and power of God over against the background of God's righteous law, man's sin and guilt, and his desperate need and insufficiency".[4] "What we need above all", he writes, "is a 'return to religion' by the way of the recovery of an effective personal evangelism, or, better perhaps, through the discovery of a still vitally Christian evangelism and evangelicalism adapted to our times and the peculiar situation which exists today".[5] "We have no reason to doubt the great value of the definite, conscious, memorable experience and act . . . of Christian conversion".[6]

In his youth, Macintosh writes, he engaged in many passionate defenses of certain "fundamentalistic" features of his faith, and his early preaching was strictly evangelistic. After two years of teaching following his graduation from high school, he spent several years on a western Ontario mission field and elsewhere in evangelistic work. Then, at McMaster University, his study of Darwin, of James' psychology, and of Mill's logic led him to become "an old-fashioned empiricist and phenomenalist" in philosophy and an "agnostic" in philosophy of religion, though his personal religious convictions remained firm, being based upon "faith". But a further study of and reflection upon the notion of the "will-to-believe" in James' thought, along with a study of W. N. Clarke's theological writings, began to lead him in the direction of a "Christian empiricism". Then a study of T. H. Greene and of Lotze made him a neo-Hegelian in philosophy; and, though he had not at that time read Royce, his teacher told him that he seemed to have "stumbled into" Royce's position. He remained an idealist until he went to the University of Chicago a few years later to "see what the new theology was", intending eventually to reach Harvard, where he would study with James and Royce.

But he soon found himself partially won over instead to the views of the "Chicago School". Dewey had just left, but Tufts, Mead, Angell, Moore, and Ames were there, as well as Burton, Mathews, Foster, and G. B. Smith in Bible and theology. Under these influences he became more or less pragmatic in his philosophy and Ritschlian in his theology. However, he was not wholly satisfied with the "anti-intellectualism" of pragmatism and the anti-metaphysical character of Ritschlianism, so h. set to work on the development of a system which could do justice to all of these elements.[7] The chief problem of modern philosophy as he saw it in 1910 is

> how to retain the ethical and religious values for which theistic personal idealism stands, together with the common-sense of realism and the new insights made possible by the functional psychology which is fundamental to the instrumental logic of the most fruitful kind of pragmatism.[8]

His own system, as we shall see, embodies an attempt to accomplish this task also. Apart from two years at Brandon College, his academic career has centered at Yale, where he has stimulated the thought of many of the most influential leaders of contemporary American Protestantism.

Macintosh's conception of theology as an empirical science is based, as we have suggested, upon a particular view of the character and significance of a certain type of religious knowledge. His theory of religious knowledge, furthermore, is closely bound up with his general theory of knowledge, and it is with respect to this fundamental issue that he disagrees most sharply with the idealistic empiricists. It is therefore necessary first to examine in some detail his general epistemological theory, in order to present and evaluate his views of religious knowledge and empirical theology with greater clarity. For the central problem of both general and religious philosophy, according to him, is the problem of knowledge. And it is of special significance in religious philosophy because, whereas, the natural scientist or sociologist may remain tentative and cautious concerning the possibility of adequately knowing the object of their inquiries, man's acting religiously depends primarily upon his views concerning the possibility of knowing God. "In the last analysis, the value of religious epistemology is the value of religion itself".[9] With the further conviction that epistemology is more than a "descriptive" enterprise and that the possibility of knowing cannot be assumed,[10] he has devoted a large part of his philosophical labor to the construction of a theory of knowledge which can avoid the pitfalls of subjectivism into which both idealism and traditional formulations of pragmatism seem to him to fall.

All idealism is incurably psychologistic, he believes. Mystical idealism

'rests upon no more stable foundation than the notion that what elapses
rom consciousness in a special state of mind is thereby shown to be un-
eal". Logical or Platonic idealism confuses the functional value of pred-
cates with the reality of subjects; and "psychological" or modern idealism
ests upon false inferences from the "subjectivity of illusion to the subjectiv-
:y of all experience".[11] Hocking's system, he believes, combines all three
orms: "if there is anything of permanent value in theoretical idealism, it
iust surely be either expressed or implied in Hocking's philosophy". But
ie *"fons et origo mali"* of his system lies in the "dogmatic" realism of the
rst step in his dialectic, which posits the same type of "objective" refer-
ice for secondary as for primary qualities. Then the transition from the
bjectivity to the subjectivity of all reality follows because he also confuses
physical experience" with "physical existence". The subsequent appeal to
ther Mind is inevitable once these two unwarranted steps are taken, while
ie appeal to "feeling" is hardly effective, in that its verification depends
pon practical experience. The "empirical" rendering of the ontological
·gument is valid only if one grants that idea is object; even so, the idea
: Other Mind would not necessarily involve an inner experience of such
a entity.[12]

Brightman's appeal to "coherence" also rests upon the subjectivist iden-
fication of idea with reality, and hence of the rational with the real, he
ys. The fact that part of reality is rational does not imply that rationality
constitutive of the whole. Furthermore, this type of idealism leads log-
ally either to rigid monism or to solipsism; if any part of the world de-
:nds for its reality upon one subject, then the idea of a *universe* means
iat ultimately there can only be one subject or Subject, in the strict sense
the term. While the personalists insist upon the independent reality of
l persons, this insight is "really derived from common human experience,
oral consciousness, and religion"; and, though Brightman and Knudson
peal to religious values in supporting their position, "they fail to bring
it clearly just what the logical relation of their metaphysical doctrine is
the religious values; they seem to think that the values support the whole
item of personalism, and they still employ the unconvincing and specula-
e arguments of Lotze and Bowne."[13]

At the same time, Macintosh feels that the functionalism of James, de-
loped by Dewey and employed, as we have seen, by Boodin, is either
ibiguous or a "disguised idealism". In treating consciousness and its con-
it as contexts of "experience" the functionalists beg the question whether
n-experienced objects exist.[14] Neorealism, on the other hand, "is the
nt product of a further disguise of disguised psychological idealism on
: one hand and disguised logical idealism on the other". That is, it apes the "subjectivist fallacy" to the subject rather than to the object.[15]

Yet any form of epistemological dualism must ultimately be agnostic, Macintosh believes. Though his own view is similar in many respects to that of the "critical realists", in that he believes in some qualitative duality of percept and object, nevertheless he cannot accept an *absolute* duality. The dualists assume immediate knowledge of the psychical only, but on this theory one could "know" one psychical state only as presented in another, and the immediately presented "would forever be simply what we try to know *with*, never what we try to know". They overlook the possibility that "just because there is such a thing as immediate knowledge . . . mediate knowledge becomes possible at all".[16]

That view which seeks to preserve at once some qualitative duality of percept and object, the insights of functionalism into the creative role of the perceiver, and the certainty which springs from numerical identity of percept and object in valid cognition is described by Macintosh as "critical realistic epistemological monism".

> By this is meant the doctrine that the object perceived is existentially, or numerically, identical with the real object at the moment of perception, although the real object may have qualities that are not perceived at that moment; and also that this same object may exist when unperceived, although *not necessarily with all the qualities it possesses when perceived*.[17]

Knowledge is ". . . certainty of the nature of reality, either in its immediate givenness or in true judgments, sufficient for all practical purposes" ". . . subjective certitude critical enough to become objective certainty".[18]

The theory of perception involved in this view is also significant for his theory of religious knowledge. Sensation, Macintosh holds, is the result of creative activity on the part of the subject, resulting from stimulation originating in environmental objects, and is definitely enough located in public space-time to be objective "for practical purposes". Consciousness is an essentially productive activity; the "primary" qualities are "revealed" through the secondary to be spatially and temporally located and, as "truly immediate", "clearly distinguishable from objects not thus present". A thing in its primary qualitative aspects may thus persist through the flux of perceived secondary qualities. Thus percepts are not totally "blind" apart from concepts, though concepts without percepts are truly "empty". Primitive cognition is perceptual.[19] Furthermore, all perception is said to occur in a "complex", and Macintosh uses the term "perception" to cover the cognition of such "objects" as change, life, selfhood, "processes of imagination", and even conception itself! Such perceptions are equivalent, he says to "perceptual intuitions". Though there is no wholly "pure" experience as described by Bergson, there are many hypotheses so long embedded in experience that they are "immediately perceived" to be true in certain situations. Thus there is an intuitive awareness of our psychical activities and of that for which they are responsible, of primary qualities, and of values.[20] Intuition may be rational, appreciative, imaginal, or perceptive; it may embrace axiomatic truths and intrinsic values as well as "reality not presented sufficiently for perception . . . needing to be tested in further perceptual intuition".

> We apprehend such processes as walking . . . in various complexes of sensory and other elements of experience; and we also *apprehend empirically*, or *perceive,* such psychical processes as perceiving, remembering, and desiring, in various complexes of elemental *sensa,* received images and constructs.[21]

Thus Macintosh can say that "broadly speaking, all cognition is, ultimately and fundamentally . . . always perceptual".[22]

This broad use of the term "perception" is, as we shall see, a crucial feature of Macintosh's claim that theology may be an empirical science, based upon religious perceptions; it is a key to his understanding of "experience". We may suggest at this point that such a view perhaps illustrates again the "fallacy of the suppressed correlative" which we have found to characterize the empiricism of the idealists, particularly Brightman, in a different manner. For when one speaks of "perceiving" perceptions and concepts, the term is being used so loosely and inclusively as to render it synonymous with cognition itself, which Macintosh admits. If conceptual and volitional and valuational elements are as significant as what are more usually termed the perceptual in this view, then it is, to say the least, ambiguous and arbitrary to insist upon calling the entire "complex" perceptual and hence material for inductive investigation.

But apart from this general difficulty there appear to be other technical shortcomings. If the primary qualities which Macintosh holds to be existent independently of cognition are "revealed" to be so in "immediate experience" of *secondary* qualities, all of which, it must be presumed, are "real" elements of gross experience, then it is difficult to see why the "primary" are of more significance, cognitively or ontologically, than the "secondary". As we shall note, the sole basis for such a distinction seems to be functional; this being so, what virtue is there in hypostatizing the experiential constancy and efficacy of the primary qualities and claiming for them independent "existence"? Does this not mean that Macintosh is really applying the old psychologistic subject-object or percept-object dichotomy to that gross experience which alone constitutes the subject-matter of operational epistemology, *in order to avoid the very difficulties* which such a presupposition leads him to find in the views of James and Dewey? Their views could hardly be called "disguised idealism" if one took seriously their claim that the very presupposition of an absolute subject-object or percept-object dichotomy in experience gives rise to all the traditional subjectivist-objectivist confusions. To say that James and Dewey "beg the question" is to indicate that the question is a live one to the critic; and this is interesting in light of the fact that the critic himself, in order to vindicate his claim that "realism" demands such a dichotomy, turns to the functionalism which he criticizes for support. For it should be noted that the "numerical" identity of which he speaks is an "identity" "for all practical purposes", and knowledge is "certainty . . . for all practical purposes . . . subjective certitude critical enough to become objective certainty". It is also interesting to note that, like Brightman, Macintosh is led to hold that the independent existence of the physical world is not theoretically but only practically certain. The "average person" in hourly adjustment to physical things knows that "practically speaking" the transcendent reality of the external physical world is "about as indubitable as his own experience or that of other persons. . . . And who shall say that this is not knowledge? . . . It is not claimed here that we know that we know. . . . Epistemology claims to be no more than the most reasonable *theory* as to the validity of human knowledge".[23]

Yet, as we noted at the outset, Macintosh maintains that realistic epistemology can find certainty in perception as well as at the end of the knowledge-process, whereas in reality the "certainty" discovered at both poles is that of some form of "intuition", or "common sense".

This statement seems warranted in the light of his account of the functional *method* of verification to which he appeals. He defines "essential pragmatism" as distinct from what he takes to be spurious formulations, as that view which "takes as its working hypothesis in logical theory the suggestion that the true test of truth is ultimately practical . . . the results of mere speculation being problematic until verified in the experiences of life".[24] James' simple identification of truth with function leaves "truth" so ambiguous as to deprive it of practical significance, he says; it does not account for truths now true but not yet verified, or for "correct guesses", and it incorrectly claims that all truth is temporary and mutable.[25] The "intellectualist" is right as over against the pragmatist in maintaining that the particular practical purpose of a judgment may be satisfied without the judgment's thereby being rendered true; nevertheless, the "identity" which the intellectualist demands is ultimately a practical identity. Thus Macintosh maintains that "the mark of truth is some sort of degree of practical identity of the idea with reality, of the predicate with the subject. And so at the heart of the good essence of pragmatism we find representationalism, the good essence of intellectualism". Such a view he calls "representational pragmatism". It differs from ordinary pragmatism, he thinks, not only in its realism but also in recognizing that ends as well as means are subject to critical examination, and in recognizing the "ideal" element in truth, "making truth in its higher reaches almost a *moral achievement*".[26]

Yet this formulation fails to yield the *certainty* which Macintosh accuses traditional pragmatism of excluding. He sees this difficulty himself and makes a further appeal, beyond the functional criterion as normally used, to "intuition". And he says that this further appeal is also in harmony with scientific method. The difficulties of representational pragmatism are to be overcome through the intuited certainty of "immediate experience and appreciation", just as scientific verification issues in a *"perception"* of the truth of its hypotheses after experimental verification. Thus the appeal to "perceptual intuition" is "the procedure of science become conscious of its own fundamental nature". Science alone adequately combines the intellectual formulation of judgments, the practical test of subject-predicate identity, and "immediate experience" as the final source of certainty.[27]

Scientific method is neither purely inductive nor purely deductive. Rationalistic postulate-systems which are only hypothetically true must be employed, since descriptive inductions must be interpreted in terms of such hypotheses. However, since the correct application of an hypothesis to inductive data is a matter of "intuition", finally; that is, since one must "see" that it is truly pertinent, it may be said that "all significant deduction is virtually induction".[28] This means that Macintosh interprets scientific or empirical method as being primarily inductive, but that he believes that induction itself, when interpreted liberally, may yield certainty. Thus he differs significantly from those who would hold that empirical method is not simply inductive but "hypothetico-inductive".

And thus it further appears that, with reference to *method* of verification as with reference to the conception of *experience,* Macintosh claims "empirical" and "scientific" sanction for his views primarily by extending these terms to cover virtually any possible sort of cognition and verification. But is it true that scientific method as normally employed derives its ultimate certainty from some sort of "intuitive" grasping of truth? Indeed, is the methodology of working science concerned with attaining the type of certainty which Macintosh seems to have in mind? Is not part of its genius the openness and caution which characterizes operationalism in general but which Macintosh criticizes as making truth "mutable" and demanding a further "intuition" of certainty? We note that our philosopher makes frequent and ambiguous use of the term "intuition", applying it alike to the "hunch" with which new hypotheses are apprehended, to the final sure "perception" of their truth *after* experimental verification, and, as we shall see, to such cognitions as the apprehension of "ideal values" in religious perception. It is the significance of the latter two usages with which we are primarily concerned. Do they actually indicate a kind of "certainty" which goes beyond the functional ideal which they are supposed to supplement? If so, is this certainty public or is it subjective; and, if it is public, does it rest ultimately upon other criteria for its vindication? These, we hold, are crucial questions for Macintosh's conception of theology as an empirical science.

As suggested above, the character of his total view seems to be compatible with a broad appeal to "common-sense", to the unquestioned certainty with which "right-thinking" individuals "perceive", i.e., "see", certain elementary truths of common experience. A former student of Macintosh has correctly indicated the kinship of this view with the Scottish Common-Sense school; Macintosh does not deny the similarities, but states that the affinities are purely coincidental.[29] He has said that both philosophy and science are, at their best, simply "critical common-sense", and that "common perception and common reflection, with their 'common-sense' results, having survived thus far in the struggle for existence by virtue of their confirmation in practical life, are for this reason to be regarded as very probably . . . essentially true".[30] The question which we shall raise as we examine his view of religious knowledge, then, is whether the "sense" which finally verifies a specific type of "religious perception" is the "common-sense" either of science or of elementary gross experience.

For the criteria of religious knowledge are broadly the same as those for knowledge in general, in Macintosh's system.[31] The refutation of mystical claims to religious knowledge is based upon the view that mysticism is fundamentally psychologistic and mistakes the character of certain unique states of consciousness for the character of their object. In all cases mystical certitude must be tested by further experience, particularly moral. Hocking's appeal to mysticism is subjected to most of the criticisms mentioned in the first chapter of this essay; in addition Macintosh claims that the term "experience" is arbitrarily restricted by Hocking, and that it should be broadened to include certain volitional factors.[32] Religious psychologists and humanists are guilty of arbitrarily confusing the subjectivity of the God-*idea* with its ontological status, of identifying psychology with ontology. What is needed is a religious realism which will defend the objectivity of its referent in roughly the same manner that "critical realistic epistemological monism" defends the objectivity of cognitive referents in general.

In the case of religious knowledge the appeal is to religious perception or experience; thus the insights of Schleiermacher must be added to those of Ritschl. Insisting upon the "autonomy of the religious consciousness" Schleiermacher became "the founder of modern theology", Macintosh says. He "made a great and lasting contribution in his *magnum opus, Die Glau-*

benslehre, a genuine normative science of the Christian faith".[33] He is to be chiefly criticised for exaggerating the autonomy of religion and not allowing for the guiding influences of science and "rational-empirical philosophy". Furthermore, his emphasis upon feeling was one-sided, and he was too anthropocentric. Ritschl, on the other hand, while offering an excellent delineation of "essential Christianity", appealed too naïvely to intuitive certainty or revelation and offered no basis for the scientific defense of value-judgments as existential.[34]

Macintosh holds that existence-judgments cannot be directly derived from value-judgments, but may be reasonably postulated thereby for further verification in experience. Thus religious knowledge "includes adequate and adequately critical (i.e. logical) certitude of the validity of ideals or values appreciated as divine (i.e. as worthy of universal human devotion) and a similar certainty . . . of the trueness of religious judgments (i.e. judgments about the divineness of reality or value, or about the reality of the divine)."[35] Value, according to him, is "a quality which anything has by virtue of its being related to an end-directed process", and values may be classified as instrumental, intrinsic, and "fundamental", the latter being the "values" inherent in value-achievement as such.[36] Divine values are, in turn, those which "may reasonably be regarded as valid ends, everywhere and for all persons", such as "rationality, beauty, goodness of personal life, individual and social"; as such they are rather "flying goals" than static perfections.[37]

But how are "fundamental" or "terminal" values to be determined? If value itself is adjectival and always relative to teleological processes, can the ends of such processes alone be called "values" also? In Macintosh's theory they are; he says that the "value" of a value-process is to be determined in relation to its end, while the value of the end is to be determined in terms of the process which leads toward it. This formulation, we may suggest, results in a certain ambiguity and circularity in value-theory as such, a circularity which is further reflected in his general theory of religious knowledge.

In any event, the most inclusive and "absolutely valid" value or end is seen by him to be "the spiritual perfection and greatest possible ultimate well-being of personality, that is, of all persons". And "the taking of such an end, or process, or value, as absolute, involves appreciative intuition". Divine values are "intuited" to be such, in a specific kind of "appreciative perception" accompanied by a sense of the "numinous", that is of the holiness of such values. The validity of this further recourse to intuition is justified by the assertion that at least one "value", namely "truth-value", must be intuitively apprehended as "valid" if the cognitive enterprise itself is to be meaningful.[38] Now many would question this use of the term "truth-value" and would maintain further that, even if such usage were legitimate, the acceptance of the "value" of truth and the acceptance of a complex "inclusive" ethical norm are not analogous cases. Surely the basing of such an over-all norm upon "intuition" makes a very significant type of decision dubiously arbitrary, in the long run, since a genuinely empirical survey of human conduct would reveal a conflicting variety of such "intuited" norms effective in human history. As we shall suggest later, Macintosh seems actually to be presupposing a "universal" intuition of certain values which would actually be accepted, more or less without question, as a matter of "common-sense" only by certain people in certain cultures, or, more specifically, within a certain religious tradition.

However, Macintosh does not base his theory of religious knowledge upon the validity of certain "appreciative perceptions" of divine values alone; he holds, rather, that "existence-judgments" may be made regarding the religious object only upon the basis of experimental "adjustment" in life to such values, an adjustment whose results may be accurately predicted and verified and which reveals an objectively divine "factor" at work in the religious and moral transformation of human character. Such adjustment constitutes "religious perception" which, like all perception, is "perception in a complex . . . the empirical intuition or perception of actual process and participating existential cause". Religious experience is not that which remains unaccounted for after moral, social, and other environmental factors have been discounted; rather it is the total experience of certain values cast in a framework of "religious realism". From the "subjective" side such experience yields the data for normative psychology of religion, and from the "objective" side it yields the data for scientifically empirical theology.[39] The religious object is thus seen to be that reality which is related to the emergence of divine values, as a "factor" in "right religious adjustment". "In the complex of divine processes we intuit, perceive, or apprehend the presence and activity of a divine factor. Empirical awareness of this divinely functioning reality we may call religious perception or religio-empirical intuition".[40]

Thus we see how Macintosh places his view of religious perception within the framework of his general theory of knowledge. Indeed, it could be asked whether the development of his theory of knowledge itself, involving as it does certain unique positions, is not perhaps in part designed to afford a philosophical foundation for the defense of the perceptual and cognitive status of a certain type of religious experience. In any event, his theory of religious knowledge embodies in its sphere the essential features of "critical monistic epistemological realism". This means, as we have seen, that there is a core of "numerical identity" of percept and object in cases of valid cognition. Many questions may of course be raised with reference to just what such "identity" means in the case of religious or any other kind of knowledge.[41] How is one to determine the extent of such "identity", and how is one to *know* that the object possesses characteristics which are not so experienced? In other words, to what extent and in what sense is God as the object of "religious perception" transcendent, or if he is transcendent how are his transcendent characteristics known? These are questions of some importance, it would seem, for the religious life; Macintosh feels, however, that it is sufficient to assert in this connection that there is enough "overlapping" of percept and object "for the practical purposes" involved.[42]

The "right" religious adjustment from which is derived that religious knowledge upon which an empirical theology may build involves concentration of the attention upon moral and spiritual ends and upon God as a hypothetically objective promoter of such values; a self-surrender to this object followed by appropriating faith, active response; and "persistence long enough and wholeheartedly enough to bring the desired result or its equivalent".[43] More specifically, it is "that adjustment to the religious object which is necessary in order to realize those values for the sake of which individuals are and ought to be experimentally religious". And "it is the religious example of Jesus which we find especially illuminating at this point".[44] It is the right religious adjustment which constitutes the heart of true prayer; just as man has learned to "adjust" to those laws of nature and society which make for his well-being through scientific trial-and-error processes, so "our prayer-life should be such as will stand the test of the most critical thought. . . . Religious adjustment is like scientific adjustment, a trial-and-error process. The right religious adjustment is the prayer attitude which works, which is dependably successful".[45]

> Prayer as the right religious adjustment is a *right* turning to Supreme Reality for the realization of Supreme Value . . . fundamentally and essentially, absolute self-surrender to God. This involves wholehearted self-commitment to the ideal of the highest attainable sincerity and purity of motive, unselfish love, courage and self-control, and whatever other qualities make up the ideal of ethical personal religion . . . involving . . . repentance and faith . . . and persistence.[46]

The knowledge of God which is derived through such experimental adjustment is thus as certain as is that established in any other type of scientific inquiry, says Macintosh. Though it is not as precisely accurate or as universally accepted as are some other scientific insights as yet, it will become more so as experimental religion progresses.[47] The results arrived at by those men and women through the ages who have conducted such religious "experiments" are at least as significant as are the results of any other experiments, especially since so many in different ages have arrived at essentially the same "conclusions". Furthermore, the religious experiment is reproducible and predictable, as is witnessed by the fact that those who have followed the directions of "experts" in the religious life have had essentially the same experiences and results.[48] Therefore the data afforded in "religious perception", through the experimental employment of the "right religious adjustment", furnish a scientifically valid foundation for the construction of theology as an empirical science.

But we may note at this point certain significant features of this view of religious experience and knowledge, before indicating further its relation to the enterprise of empirical theology as such. It is evident that the really crucial feature is the appeal to the intuitive appreciation or "perception" of certain values as divine, and we have already raised certain questions about this type of appeal. But the further question arises whether any "perception-in-a-complex" in which complex but specific value-judgments of the type ascribed by Macintosh to "religious perception" may be called "scientific". It is evident that such perception is colored by personal commitments to certain ideals chiefly associated with a certain religious tradition. What is more usually called scientific perception is characterized rather by a type of "objectivity" and "disinterestedness", at least as an ideal, which would seem inappropriate to the type of experience which Macintosh describes. Furthermore, the purpose of scientific experiment is to furnish a reliable basis for the operational understanding and control of defined areas of experience; it involves not simply a passive "adjustment" to laws of nature, but an active manipulation by man of selected bits of his environment in the interest of specific human goals, an "exploitation" of his world for human ends. The character of nature is thereby altered, for good or for ill; that is, in scientific experiment man learns how to change or manipulate certain forces which constitute the "objects" of such experiment, as well as to "adjust" to others. But Macintosh writes that "prayer, as surrender to God, contemplates a change, not in God but in man—a change in man through a changed relation to God, and a change in things through the change which thus takes place in man".[49] Thus the "adjustment" is not of the same character as scientific "adjustment"; its aim is surrender, not control; in "true prayer" as thus described man seeks to *be* controlled *by* an extra-human if not supernatural "factor" rather than to adjust to or control natural forces for preconceived and definite human ends. The use of the term "factor" in this connection suggests similar ambiguities.

Furthermore, scientific experiment or "perception" usually points to carefully defined types of public experience as the locus of its verification, and in such verification certain stable sensory factors are fundamental. But the "objective" element in religious perception as described by Macintosh is clearly not public or sensory in this sense, but is rather "intuitive" or else broadly behavioral, involving the consequences of such experiment in the life of the believer. And the emphasis upon "the religious example of Jesus" as "especially illuminating" in determining what the "right" religious adjustment is[50] suggests that the "universality" of such experience is the universality of one type of religious belief among others. It is true that Macintosh has recently said that "it seems to me highly desirable that we find an alternative to the Christocentric theology and theological methodology" and that "if Christology and the Christocentric approach make my historically skeptical brother stumble, I will no longer insist that the essentials of religion be always clothed in these . . . concepts".[51] Nevertheless one alternative which he suggests is simply to

> find confirmation for our appreciations and for what tends to be our faith when we are spiritually at our best, by appealing to the spiritual judgment and faith of Jesus, whose spiritual vision was presumably the clearest to be found among men, as his life was presumably the best. . . . We could say that we have in the religious experience of Jesus our best illustration . . . of what God, in the sense of a divinely functioning Reality and Cause, can do. . . . This would be an exceedingly important datum for a realistic empirical theology.[52]

Or, he says,

> the Christian gospel can stand on its own merits, without being heralded either as a gospel of Jesus or . . . about Jesus. . . . We have then the eternally valid social ideal of the reign of God's righteous will in human society, with the good news that if adequate resources be made of divine help, the ideal . . . will prove feasible and progressively realisable. . . . He who honestly follows this course . . . will also begin to understand the traditional figure of Jesus better, as one who in his own historical situation was so fully indwelt by the divine spirit . . . as to rightly have a certain normative function in the spiritual lives of later individuals.[53]

Thus in any case it is an essentially Christian experience which Macintosh has in mind when he speaks of "the right religious adjustment", an experience which includes the type of Christian conversion, which, as we have seen, has been of chief significance in Macintosh's own religious life and which if reinterpreted in the light of modern knowledge and emphases, he would use as the basis for a new Christian evangelicalism. Is such experience then "universal" in the scientific sense? Would it be possible for one who "intuited" different values to have such an experience, or to be convinced of its "authenticity" when its results for life and conduct were demonstrated in "religious experiment"? It can only be concluded that the universality and "certainty" associated with such experience is the certainty and universality of the "common sense" of a given tradition, not the common sense to which what are usually termed scientific experiments appeal.

We shall have occasion to return to this point later; let us now, however, see how Macintosh would build an empirical theology. "On the basis of religious perception," he says, "it ought to be and indeed is possible to formulate empirical laws as to what a dependable and divinely functioning reality can be depended upon for, under stated specific conditions of religious adjustment".[54] Theological theory should be related to religious experience as physical or social theory are related to physical and social experience. Thus the following steps would lead to the establishment of theology as an empirical science:

First, there should be a formal definition of the "subject-matter", God, perhaps in terms of "the ultimate object of religious dependence", whose specific attributes are to be discovered in the scientific analysis of religious experience. Then there would be a statement of general "presuppositions". These would include adherence to "the laws of thought"; an acceptance of "the established results of other sciences"; an acknowledgement of the possibility of freedom and immortality insofar as this may be inferred from non-religious knowledge; data indicating the human consequences of "evil and sin" as discoverable "apart from religion"; and, finally, the "peculiar" presupposition of theology, namely the hypothetical existence of its object, God, as possessing certain characteristics.[55]

Though it would seem that there is considerable presumption in the use of such a term as "the established results of other sciences", Macintosh believes that such "results" definitely imply belief in cosmic evolution and in the law of entropy as well as an "electrical" view of matter in physics; and a general application of the evolutionary hypothesis in biology and, with modifications, in morals, religion, and aesthetics. A further "established" result which is of some significance for his system is the historicity of Jesus, though he has held, from time to time, slightly different views as to just how important this "datum" is. In general he seems now to hold that

> there is an *essential* identity, that is, an identity sufficient for practical religious purposes between the Christ of faith and the actual Jesus of history. I hold this not to be so much logically indispensable for an essentially Christian faith . . . as historically indispensable for a reasonable explanation of the genesis of the Christian religion.[56]

Presupposition of freedom of the will is defended on the grounds that the spontaneity of physical and moral activity demands it, and the possibility of immortality is held to be not only morally desirable but also theo-

retically possible in the light of physical and psychical research. Consequences of "sin and evil" are seen in social and economic losses. And the
"peculiar" presupposition of theology is postulated on the basis of "pre-
scientific experience" in "religious intuition" of some Object upon which
depends moral deliverance—an experience analogous to the botanist's
"prescientific" experience of plants. Macintosh has subsequently admitted
that many people probably have no such "prescientific" experience of the
Object as conceived by him, or perhaps no articulated experience of any
religious object at all. But beyond this, it must be asked whether the entertaining of such a "presupposition" in "theology as an empirical science",
resting as it does upon a "religious intuition" which is later to become part
of the data for "scientific" analysis, does not make the whole enterprise circular.[57]

With these presuppositions empirical theology is to turn to the data afforded by religious experience, "religious apperception", or "revelation",
these being synonymous terms. But not all such experiences afford a suitable "subject-matter". "Some religious experience, operating with faulty
hypotheses as to the nature and activity of God, has value only in showing
what God is not and does not do". The proper selection of the data for
theology "presupposes sufficient progress in religious discrimination to be
able to distinguish the distinctively divine elements within human experience". And such discrimination is made, again, on the basis of "religious
apperception". That is, we recognize the authenticity of the subject-matter
because its quality is what, in the course of experience, we have found to
be characteristic of the "true" religious object *through the religious experience of ourselves and of others in a given tradition!* The distinction between valid and invalid religious perception "has long been recognized by
prophets, apostles, theologians, pastors, missionaries, and evangelists".[58]
Though "revelation is presumably as universal as experimental religion
of any spiritual value", nevertheless, "within the limits of experimental
religion the most normative revelation of the divine is to be found, apparently, in the personal life and character of Jesus, the 'Christ', in his 'aton-
ing' work, in the resultant Christian experience of 'salvation', and in the
developing 'Kingdom of God' ".[59] The reasons for this selective narrowing
of the data by Macintosh are not elaborated. Perhaps they are bound up
with the notion of "religious apperception" in his general theory of religious knowledge, which, as we have suggested, ultimately appeals for its
justification to Christian "common-sense". Jesus is said to afford the clearest example of the "right religious adjustment"; on the other hand, such an
adjustment is said to be "right" because it promotes those values "perceived" by Christians to be divine.

Having limited the data to Christian forms, Macintosh proceeds to formulate the "laws" of empirical theology: There are the laws of "elemental experiences" or of the answer to prayer", including the law of receiving moral power for repentance, and moral aspiration, for self-control and courage, for victory over temptation, and so on. Then there are further laws of "composite experiences" of which the most important are, "to use the traditional terms, 'regeneration', 'perseverance', 'fulness of the spirit', and 'sanctification' ". Secondary theological laws, dealing with primarily emotional rather than volitional results of religious experience, include "the law of the feeling of repentance", of "Christian peace", "Christian joy", and "Christian love". Laws of "intellectual" experiences deal with such matters as "divine guidance" and "assurance" or "the witness of the Spirit". Other secondary "laws" are physiological and sociological in import. Each law is precisely formulated and categorized, a recent formulation employing alphabetical symbols in scientific style. It is not necessary to list here the complete table in detail.[60]

Now strictly "empirical" theology is limited in its function to the formulation of such laws and the resulting "fully verifiable" statements, according to Macintosh. Metaphysical and cosmological implications may be found, but the construction of systems of metaphysics involves speculative activity which takes one beyond the realm of the strictly empirical. Thus he would differ sharply with our idealists who find sweeping metaphysical doctrines "empirically given" in various types of experience. "Reasonable postulates" alone emerge from the empirical subject-matter of theology, says Macintosh, though these must be taken account of in any complete system of metaphysics. Such "reasonable postulates" are also coupled with "unrefuted overbeliefs" suggested by "religious tradition at its best" to form the substance of what Macintosh calls "normative" or "theoretical" theology, in which various doctrines are stated more exhaustively, but in speculative terms.[61]

Now we have already suggested that, in practice, Macintosh really presupposes many of the insights of "normative" or "valuational" theology in what he takes to be the strictly "empirical" part of the whole enterprise. In his theory of religious knowledge a specific type of experience is held to be "valid" on the grounds that "religious apperception" justifies the claim. In the development of the empirical theology based thereon the selection of relevant data is dependent upon the same type of discrimination, while at the same time a "presupposition" of the entire enterprise is the existence of its specific object, the postulate of a specific value-judgment. Furthermore, in the formulation of the "laws", and in the description of religious perception, one qualifying characteristic is "persistence until the desired result or its equivalent has been achieved". Could such a requirement conceivably be a qualification of what is more normally called scientific experiment? Is it not a further illustration of the fact that the "empirical" aspect of Macintosh's theology is little more than an inevitable outcome or counterpart of the "apperception" of certain religious values as supreme? Do the findings of empirical theology as understood by him mean more than that, if one "intuits", "apperceives", "perceives", or chooses "on faith" to act upon certain value-hypotheses, then certain results follow? Are the hypotheses themselves thereby proved valid or invalid, since the worth of the results is itself to be decided in terms of value-judgments? The "right" religious adjustment surely cannot itself establish the validity of the criteria in terms of which its own "rightness" is delineated.

Thus we should agree with other criticis of Macintosh's position that, while he seeks to supplement valuational with empirical theology, Ritschl with Schleiermacher, his system is *primarily* valuational and secondarily empirical or "existential" as he understands the latter term.[62] While he criticizes Brightman's appeal to value-experience as "confusing the reality which has value with the value which the reality has", thus making the transition from the appreciation of religious values to the statement that the religious object exists too simple, it seems doubtful whether Macintosh's insertion of the "empirical" element actually alters the procedure to any great extent.

That his theological emphasis is primarily upon valuational analysis is also evident from some of his popular writings which followed the publication of *Theology as an Empirical Science*. In his Bross Prize volume he states that if some values are established as "valid" they become legitimate bases of inference concerning the nature of reality.[63] A consquence of this assertion is his emphasis, in this and subsequent volumes, upon the philosophical significance of that attitude which he calls "moral optimism"—"a fundamental attitude of confidence in the cosmos, together with a full sense of man's responsibility", the healthy-minded attitude which assures "inner or spiritual preparedness for anything the future can bring".[64] It is "the optimism of the healthy mind in the healthy body and . . . the good or moral will"; and it is significant for religious philosophy because it seems reasonable to believe what we need to believe in order to live as we ought— that is, with moral optimism. "That idea which is theoretically permissible in the light of all we know, and which seems at the same time practically necessary for the realization of our purposes, is likely to appeal to us as probably true". The affinity with James' "will-to-believe" is recognized, though Macintosh says that what he means is rather "belief itself".[65]

Interestingly enough, Macintosh himself has suggested many limitations and qualifications for this type of approach. In an early volume he stated that it is "far from achieving logical verification for its doctrines" and is, in general, "too subjective to become completely satisfactory".[66] More lately, he has declared that since writing *The Reasonableness of Christianity* he has concluded that "moral optimism" *follows from* and therefore cannot be made the basis of an "argument" which is designed to bring one to a basic Christian experience:

> It would seem . . . that the surest way of achieving the essentially Christian faith which is involved in moral optimism . . . is not to try to reason one's self into moral optimism simply, but to *become* a moral optimist by having the Christian religious experience.[67]

To the writer this analysis seems justified, but it also seems to be a significant admission of a difficulty inherent in his total view of "empirical" theology as well. We have seen that he conceives "empirical method" as combining intellectual certainty, valuational intuition, and functional verification. But if he admits that the appeal to the functional implications of a certain attitude itself presupposes a more complex total experience and commitment, and that the ultimate basis of certainty in religious perception is also "intuitive" or "apperceptive", then our claim that his empirical theology finally rests upon certain uncriticized but fundamental value-judgments common to a given tradition and culture seems justified.

Or, to put the matter in terms of the traditional theistic "arguments", it would seem that, while he rejects the usual formulations of the moral and ontological arguments, his "empirical argument" is actually a combination of these with certain features of the teleological. In this respect his position is perhaps nearer to those of Brightman and Wieman than any of the three indicate in their criticisms of each other. While he rejects the rationalistic rendering of the moral argument which moves by inference directly from the conscious experience of certain ideal values to the "proof" of the existence of an ideal being,[68] he holds that his empirical argument is a "complement to the moral . . . in one of its possible forms. On the basis of man's need of moral salvation, the existence of God, the moral Savior, may be postulated as humanly imperative," the verification of the postulate being dependent upon subsequent "experiment".[69] We have indicated our reasons for holding, however, that the empirical verification is itself dependent for its significance upon the basic moral "intuition" and thus we would agree with Dewey that Macintosh's case for theism is actually a specific formulation of and not a complement to the moral argument.[70] We should also maintain that the transition from an observable "factor" in certain types of moral experience to the idea of a supreme being who is the source and judge of all values, and the subsequent postulation of the "existence" of such a being, involves the essential contention of the ontological argument. He rejects the cosmological argument on the ground that a "first-cause" if postulated need not be God, though on the other hand the "cause" of the experience of moral salvation must be; the teleological argument is also held by him to be at best complementary to the "empirical".[71] That is to say, one specific type of religio-moral experience is normative in the interpretation of "reality as a whole".

In the view of God derived therefrom Macintosh rejects Brightman's claim that only a finite deity can be truly "empirical". He finds the problem of evil solved in terms of the consequences of human freedom and claims that ours is the best possible kind of world for the education and discipline of free moral agents. Many evils may be accounted for in terms of "natural causation", and the crucial religious experience of salvation makes moral evil at its worst intelligible without attributing it to a "given" element in God himself.[72] Brightman's view, he claims, is merely a result of his personalism: since for him only persons and the Supreme Person are real, and "surd" evil may be attributed to neither man nor Devil, it must be attributed to God. A non-personalist could hold that evil in the world is not now dependent upon God's consciousness but is objective to both God and man, a consequence of free creation.[73] But granting the presuppositions which give rise to the problem, Brightman seems justified in replying that dating the cause of evil back in time or making it "objective" to God's present consciousness does not relieve God of responsibility for it and its present "limiting" functions. In any case, Macintosh's treatment of the problem is indicative of a continuing emphasis in his theological theory upon a question which other empiricists might view as being itself unempirical.

God is described by Macintosh chiefly in terms of the divine value-producing "factor" in the "right religious adjustment" who educates man through cosmic processes to the acknowledgement of ideal values, "a worthy object of human devotion, love and trust . . . Holy Love." Through "imaginal intuition" we may conceive such a "factor", acting personally in the experience of salvation, as itself or Himself personal.[74] His view of the relation of God to the rest of reality he calls a "natural-supernaturalism", "having among its governing ideas an orderly universe in which there is ample room for divine and human freedom, in which also origins may be described in terms of creative evolution, and in which mechanical, vital, and humanly purposive processes may all be comprehended within one general plan", the decisively "miraculous" manifestation of the divine occurring in moral salvation.[75] In any complete metaphysic the findings of empirical theology must be taken account of along with those of other sciences, he says. And the resulting system must do justice to both substance and process, mind and matter, the one and the many, and to freedom. It may be that the most adequate way of expressing all these emphases would be to conceive of the cosmos as related to God as body to spirit. Physical and vital factors would constitute the "body", while in experimental religion "man is aware of coming into contact with the immanent divine Spirit." Human beings would thus be viewed as organs within an organism, "yet more independent than this analogy would suggest".[76]

But Macintosh insists that these metaphysical hypotheses are speculative and not strictly empirical, though they are perhaps not incompatible with the findings of empirical sciences, including theology. Nevertheless, he insists that any metaphysic which did justice to all these factors would still be more a "faith" than a scientific construction, just as there is a careful distinction to be made between the truly "empirical" and the "theoretical" elements in theology itself. But the question we have raised at various points in our exposition is whether the "empirical" element in theology as conceived by him is not also dependent upon and subordinate to valuational decisions or "perceptual intuitions" which are ultimately "decisions of faith", recognized as valid by Christian "common-sense". Are "religious perception" and the laws derivable therefrom actually universal and "scientific" in any usually accepted sense of the term?

We noted, first of all, that his theory of religious knowledge as ultimately "perceptual" and "inductive" rests upon his general theory of "perception-in-a-complex" or "perceptual intuition", which employs the term "perception" so loosely as to include by definition almost any conceivable type of cognition. On the strength of this usage he can further claim that all verification is ultimately inductive, since the rationalistic features of scientific method are "intuited" as pertinent and the certainty of the result of experiment is grasped in "perceptual intuition". And since he understands "empirical method" to mean primarily "inductive method", he can claim to be an empiricist in this respect. Hence both subject-matter and method are rendered "empirical" by definition.

Nevertheless, in his general theory of knowledge the criteria employed in the discrimination and classification of "perceptions-in-a-complex" in the various non-theological sciences are admittedly public and ultimately sensory in reference. In the case of religious perception, on the other hand, such publicly objective sensory elements are not crucial; the "complex" involves numerous volitional and moral elements, and the "certainty" is more subjective. As Professor Bixler has put it, the religious perception "turns out to be one where the new element is not knowledge but will, so that religion becomes an experience of value rather than of fact. The hands are intellectualistic but the voice is that of pragmatism".[77] And the functional aspect, in turn, rests upon an original and normative "apperception" of ideal value; hence what the theory finally amounts to is the proposition that specific religious and moral values are perceptible facts.

Now there may be some sense in which it may be said that values, or at least value-processes, are "facts". We shall wish to pursue this question further after we have indicated the role which such a supposition plays in the thought of Professor Wieman. But we would suggest here that if values are facts, they are hardly perceptible objects of the same pattern as and with criteria even analagous to those of sensory percepts. We may speak of value-processes as being "perceived" only if "perception" means something as broad as Macintosh's "perception-in-a-complex", which ultimately means simply that they are cognizable in some sense. But the "perceptual intuition" of certainty in the case of religio-ethical experience is hardly of one cloth with the "intuition" of scientific certainty—if, indeed, the goal of scientific perception and operation is the attainment of that kind of certainty which Macintosh seems to have in mind.

A similar ambiguity appears in his development of empirical theology as such. Among the "presuppositions" of such an enterprise is the existence of its object—though Macintosh has latterly admitted that the "pre-scientific intuition" of such an entity is far from universal in the sense that the common hypotheses of science or of gross experience are. Then, in the selection of the data for analysis, there is a further appeal to "religious apperception" emerging from the background of a given religious tradition. With these restrictive qualifications it seems that the "laws" revealed in the analysis are inevitable, particularly since one of the qualifications of religious "experiment" is that it must be persisted in until the desired result or its equivalent is achieved. Thus it seems evident that in each stage of Macintosh's development of an empirical theology there are restrictive and subjective appeals to certain presupposed value-judgments which could hardly be tolerated in any other empirical science.

In other words, Macintosh's system is fraught with all the difficulties which arise from the arbitrary appeal to one specific type of experience as normative in the interpretation of "the whole". Some of these were suggested in connection with Hocking's appeal to mystical experience for the empirical grounding of his objective idealism; others we shall mention in our evaluation of the movement as a whole. In general we maintain that such a restriction of the empirical *subject-matter* results in a corresponding restriction in the understanding and employment of empirical method, as much in the case of Macintosh's realism as in the case of idealism. In this instance the justification offered for the restriction is ultimately "intuitive", or based upon the dubiously autonomous "common-sense" validity of certain religious value-judgments. Though in some instances he seems to wish to broaden the empirical subject-matter to include the religious experience of variant traditions as data for the construction of a "universal" theology,[78] he makes the criteria for the selection of such experiences as may be universally valid "primarily spiritual and more particularly a result in the will, a promoting of a good and essentially *Christlike* will."[79] A more recent statement is even more revealing: "the essential truth of theology as (centrally, or fundamentally) an empirical science is logically bound up, it seems to me, with the essential truth of modern evangelical Christianity. . . . That Christianity is not essentially true it is impossible for me to believe. . . ."[80] We maintain that this appeal to the "common-sense" of a given religious tradition is different in principle from such appeal to common-sense, as may be involved in ordinary scientific experience, and that the spiritual certainty and total committment of life, characteristic of the religious experience described are incompatible with the aim of other sciences at the experimental control of their data. This last suggestion we shall elaborate in our concluding summary; we turn now to the religious philosophy of one who has sought to be more consistently "scientific" in his view of both religious perception and empirical method as employed in philosophy of religion.

II: H. N. Wieman, *Theistic Naturalist*

Henry Nelson Wieman (1884–), like the other empirical philosophers of religion who have figured in our study, began his philosophical development as an absolute idealist, embracing the teachings of Josiah Royce as presented by Silas Evans at Park College. But early in his development he became suspicious of absolutism's claims to finish truth and absolute certainty and of the popularity of idealism at that time among Christian apologists for the philosophical expression of theological doctrines. During graduate study in Europe this suspicion crystallized into formal criticism. Abroad he studied with Windelband and Troeltsch, but he found the former stimulating only as a historian and "systematizer" of thought, while he could not accept Troeltsch's emphasis upon history as being of chief significance in the formulation of a "philosophy of life". It was rather at Harvard that he found stimulation for the development of his own viewpoint in religious philosophy. There he studied with Perry and Hocking, and it is to the latter that he declares himself chiefly indebted for basic religious insights. "I distinguish sharply", he writes, "between the profound insights into the religious way of living, which Hocking reveals, and the system of philosophy in which he clothes them. In the former he is, to my mind, unsurpassed among living men".[1] Further tribute to Hocking was paid in the first major publication of Wieman's own views.[2]

Later he drew heavily upon Whitehead and Dewey in formulating a philosophy which seeks to avoid the errors which seem to him to be inherent in any idealistic framework for the expression of religious faith. Whitehead's *Process and Reality* he described as "the most magnificent achievement of constructive imagination that modern times can show", and he declares that *The Concept of Nature* and *Religion in the Making* were "exciting discoveries" in his intellectual quest.[3] J. C. Smut's "holism" has also been influential in Wieman's metaphysical views, while he has turned to Dewey's experimentalism in his methodology and in his theory of value. His pragmatic approach to epistemology has also been influenced considerably by the writings of C. I. Lewis and, indirectly, by the logical empiricists. More lately he has sought to take account, in his theological views, of the critical insights of Barth, Brunner, Tillich, and Berdyaev, and he has stressed the importance of a "theocentric" attitude in religion, declaring at the same time a new appreciation for traditional Christian symbols in the expression of faith.[4]

Like Macintosh, Wieman is critical of the restrictive subjectivism and absolutism associated with most idealistic philosophies of religion, and he has insisted that God is an independently existing object of perception, knowledge of whom is scientifically verifiable.[5] But beyond this basic realism and general devotion to "scientific method" there are many points of difference in the views of the two thinkers. These differences stem in part from different theories of knowledge and value and from different conceptions of scientific method and its exact role in the formulation of "empirical theology". There is also an essentially different view of the religious object as such and of the relation of God to nature.

Wieman has classified his view as "theistic naturalism". This means that he would avoid any ultimate separation of God from nature; that he views God as one natural process or structure of processes among others which can be apprehended in clearly defined ways with predictible results. It has been his purpose, he says, "so to formulate the idea of God that the question of God's existence becomes a dead issue".[6] To accomplish this he has offered as a "minimal" definition of God the following: "God is that something upon which human life is most dependent for its security, welfare, and increasing abundance . . . that something of supreme value which constitutes the most important conditions".[7] If God be defined as supreme value or as that process which underlies and makes possible the maximum achievement of value then the fact of his existence, if not full knowledge of his specific nature, is "inescapable", he feels. "The best there is and can be . . . is a self-proving proposition".[8] As we shall see later, Wieman has offered a number of more specific definitions of just what this supremely valuable process may be said to be, and there are a number of questions to be raised concerning these definitions. The point that we wish to make here is that he views God as a natural process, or as a structure of mutually supporting processes, which lends itself to empirical observation. Such a process or structure of processes may be superhuman but cannot be "supernatural", because nature is defined by him as "what we know through the interaction between the physiological organism and its environment" and the supernatural is unknowable by definition. Knowledge of God is derived from "a series of material impacts upon the organism" and "all knowledge gained in this way is knowledge of nature".[9]

Thus Wieman, like Macintosh, maintains that God is an object of religious perception, but he means by this something which he feels is more public and precise than "right religious adjustment". Indeed, he has at times offered detailed criticisms of any "appeal to religious experience" of specific kinds as having normative status in the formulation of religious philosophy. He has said that Christian liberals "bungled . . . in misunderstanding and misusing the empirical method" by identifying empirical theology with the appeal to religious experience.[10] The term "religious experience" is itself a "nest of ambiguities and confusion", he says. And he wrote, in a review of a volume of essays in honor of Macintosh, that he believed the critical tenor of the essays by Macintosh's former students meant that "the day of certainty of religious experience has passed. . . . Here is a smashing blow at that method of religious inquiry".[11] Subjective or social effects of crucial experiences must not be taken as final guarantees of their validity, even when these are related to currently accepted moral norms as in the case of Macintosh's "moral optimism".[12] On the other hand, Brightman's broader view of religious experience and its verification in terms of "coherence" he describes as "sterile" and tautologous, "worthless as a means to finding the reality of God". Any appeal to "coherence" is ambiguous unless it means the appeal to a coherence of purely rational concepts apart from empirical verification, he says, in which case the philosophy involved is more precisely labelled rationalistic rather than empirical.[13] Religious experience of a specific pattern, he says, expressing agreement with Dewey, "should never be set apart as being somehow God or constituting value as the rest of the world cannot, the rest of life being subordinated as a mere means to this, while this is a means to nothing else".[14]

Nevertheless Wieman has himself placed considerable emphasis upon a type of religious experience which he calls "problem-solving mysticism", as we shall see, and in a recent article he declared that the way to determine the "category" most appropriate to deity is to "render explicit by analysis the category for God which is implicit in the living of the most magnificent lives of our Christian tradition. . . . Pre-eminently exemplified in Paul".[15] However, he subsequently denied that he meant thereby to associate himself with the "religio-psychological school" of Wobbermin and others. "I repudiate the whole approach to religion by way of religious experience. One must know what God is by other criteria than the feel of the experience or the traditional character of it . . . or even the approved consequences in the form of moral character that may issue from it".[16] We have suggested briefly the manner in which he would go about determining the character of deity in terms of value and natural processes, and we shall say more about this below. First we wish to examine in greater detail what Wieman does mean by "perception" of God, in terms of his general theory of perception as such.

We have suggested that the influence of Whitehead, Dewey, and Lewis is evident in his view of experience and knowledge. In an early essay he defined experience as "the sensous qualities in that temporal and spatial structure that goes to make up nature". In experience immediately had, there is no final bifurcation of physical and psychical, noumenal and phenomenal, or of primary and secondary qualities, as other empiricists have sometimes claimed. "Mind", he says, is simply a kind of event which occurs when physical processes interact in an "overlapping" of space and time, when experience controls objects not only directly in the present but also indirectly through awareness of past and future. Concepts are "pointers" or symbols which designate objects through the medium of an associated system of habits. Conceptual "objects" may be either events of immediate experience or other concepts, as is the case in mathematico-logical systems. Logical categories are not mysteriously "a-priori" in either nature or experience; they represent rather the consciously and deliberately adopted functional grammar of thought.[17]

Gross experience is to be distinguished from knowledge, which is defined as "experience which is known to have occurred" or experience which is known to be possible under defined conditions. Experience, in other words, affords the material for knowledge, and there is no one type of experience which possesses immediate and unique cognitive value. We know objects only when we "are able to designate certain sense qualities having a certain order in space and time".[18] Meaning signifies "the method by which we control experience" and is not to be construed as either "psychical" or "physical", but rather in terms of its operations. The difference between valid and illusory experiences consists in the fact that the former are understood in a larger number of predictable relations with other experiences than are the latter; both types of experience are equally "real". The search for truth is thus the search for the most rewarding clues to the largest number of into-experiential connections. The aim of inquiry is progressively to increase the store of such connections in such a way that the experienced world is progressively "transformed".[19]

Thus Wieman agrees with Lewis in distinguishing the conceptual from the "given" in experience, viewing the latter as "a massive happening which can be investigated progressively by common sense and science". And more recently he has placed less importance upon the sensory elements in perception, which is of special significance in view of statements which he has made about God as an object of sense-perception. He has recently stressed the significance of "linguistic elements" in the perceptual complex and has modified the pragmatic emphasis on successful prediction in the delineation of truth by declaring that

> linguistic signs being used in the perceptual event (if there be such) which specify some relation between the perceptual event and others, are what is true and false. If the perception does not carry such signs, then the perception is a happening, peculiar in carrying in it psychic anticipations, fears, and aversions, which may be consummated or not. But in no case is such a mind-body event true or false without the linguistic signs specifying a structure of relations between the present event and others that have occurred in the past, along with possibilities that might be actualised in the future if certain further conditions are provided. . . . Perhaps no perceptual event occurs in human experience without linguistic signs.[20]

Thus

> the question about any object is never correctly expressed by asking: Is it perceived object or inferred object? When we perceive anything at all in such a way as to involve truth and error, it is by perceptual inference and never by perception apart from inference . . . truth and error pertain to perception only when the perception includes the affirmation or denial of a proposition with its implications and inferences.[20]

At the same time Wieman makes a distinction between "perceived object" and "perceptual event". A perceived object is "a structure of interrelated events, some of which must be perceptual events", while "perceptual event" is conceived more broadly as a "happening" that is physical, physiological, psychological, and social, but cognitive only when "linguistic signs" are operative. "The perceptual event is very complex. It includes everything which, if changed, would make a difference to the perceptual experience . . . vastly more than enters conscious awareness at the moment".[21] Thus, in terms of this broader view of "perceived object" and "perceptual event", Wieman can say that the question whether God can be perceived would be answered by determining whether there are "certain happenings occurring . . . which, when proper meanings have been developed, assume the form of perceptual events found to have that structure . . . which can be identified as the structure of creativity which generates all value".[22]

Now this broadening development in general theory of perception by Wieman bears an interesting relation, it seems to us, to his theory of religious knowledge as such. We have suggested that Macintosh's theory of knowledge and perception would be interpreted as a kind of apologetic for the significance and cognitive validity of a specific kind of religious experience; and one wonders to what extent Wieman's views of perception are also influenced by his desire to defend the thesis that God as defined by him is a "perceived object". At an early date he maintained that God must be "an object of sensuous experience" or "purely a system of concepts and nothing more". Knowledge of objects through sensory experience he termed "knowledge by acquaintance", while purely conceptual knowledge is "knowledge by description" and is of secondary cognitive value. He himself believed that it is possible to have "direct" knowledge of God "by acquaintance", through sensory perception. We shall indicate below the relation of this claim to his description of "problem-solving mysticism" in religious experience.[23] But now he seems to place more emphasis upon the role of conceptual elements in the perceptual complex, calling such elements "linguistic signs". This seems to make the (a-priori?) concept of deity a matter of primary importance in religious knowledge.

But is not this broader view of perception ambiguous at certain crucial points, namely in the description of "perceptual event" as distinguished from "perceived object", and with reference to the question whether there *are* any "perceptual events" which do not involve "linguistic signs" and are thus in some sense cognitive? Though he still maintains that some objects of knowledge may be "inferred only" and not perceived, he seems to have modified considerably the notion of "knowledge by acquaintance" in saying that all perceptual cognitions involve also inferences. And this seems to result in a blurring of the usual distinction between percept and concept to such an extent that "perception" becomes something almost as vague as Macintosh's "perception-in-a-complex". This procedure is hardly designed to clarify the central issue of the debate in religious philosophy which has centered around the question whether God may be perceived. It does not seem fruitful to defend the thesis that such religious perception is possible by progressively broadening and extending the meaning of "perception" and "perceived object".

But let us examine in greater detail just what Wieman has meant in his claim that God is the object of sensory perception. This claim, as we have suggested, is bound up in part with that emphasis upon a particular type of religious experience which, despite his criticism of other types of appeal to religious experience, seems to have played a major role in his own religious life as well as in the formulation of his religious philosophy. Indeed, a recent critic has argued rather cogently that a certain kind of mystical experience is of such importance in Wieman's faith that he could be described as a "religious mystic who has been deeply bitten by contemporary scepticism of religion and who consequently endeavors to provide a method whereby the religious skeptic can still attain the values of religion".[24] While this statement may be somewhat exaggerated, any careful examination of Wieman's religious philosophy does reveal, it seems to us, that the kind of experience which he has called "problem-solving mysticism" is of extreme importance for if not definitive in his views of the nature of God and of religious knowledge.

We have already noted Wieman's acknowledgement of his indebtedness to Hocking for major insights into the character of religious experience and the religious life. In his own descriptions of religious experience a further indebtedness to James is also apparent, and he would also relate such experience to Dewey's analyses of experience in general and of value-experience in particular. The religious experience to which he would point is the type of experience which often occurs in life-crises; it may be associated with general bewilderment in the face of apparently insoluble problems, with experiences of intense sorrow, with feelings of awe and wonder in the presence of natural beauty or grandeur, with intense emotions of love, or perhaps with religious meetings designed to bring those present to an intensely critical examination of and perhaps a definite and transforming break with their established habits of thought and action, such as the Christian evangelistic meetings emphasized by Macintosh.

Such experience is characterized by "a wild flinging about" and may issue in the spontaneous appearance of novel impulses and suggestions. It involves no immediately definable conceptual cognition but seems to be an immediate experience of "undefined awareness of total passage of nature, the undiscriminated event . . . the totality of experience which immediately flows over one".[25] If there be any meaning at all in this experience as immediately had, it is minimal; the whole seems to occur on the "threshold of consciousness" (James) at which meaning fades imperceptibly into unconsciousness. It is similar, Wieman thinks, to what Dewey calls "consciousness as a bare event". "It is experience caught in that intervening period when old meanings have faded out and new meanings have not been born . . . experience *pregnant* with meaning . . . a quivering mass of sensitivity to the total undiscriminated situation".[26]

In a volume written more directly from the background of his own religious life, Wieman has suggested certain techniques for the cultivation and utilization of "problem-solving mysticism". "It consists", he says, "in exposing oneself to the stimulation of a problematical situation with a mind freed of all bias and preconception and waiting in this state, or returning to it periodically, until there dawns upon the mind that integration which will solve the problem". He has found early morning and late evening hours, in some place of quiet solitude, most fruitful occasions for such meditation. First one seeks complete relaxation and strives for a maximum awareness of reality, and especially of "that" in reality which is of most importance for the support and increase of life and value. Then one meditates upon unfulfilled possibilities for good in one's immediate situation. Then, with this preparation, one turns to one's particular immediate problems and attempts to face them objectively, for the purpose of discovering what changes of personal habit and attitude are necessary for their solution in accord with the desire to achieve maximum good. Finally there should follow an exercise of something like auto-suggestion, in which one formulates verbally the conclusions he has reached and repeats his resolves over and over in a worshipful attitude of determination and supplication.[27]

Now Wieman agrees with Macintosh in his criticisms of most types of mystical experience, and adds his own warnings against uncritical acceptance of evidence from extraordinary experiences directly traceable to bodily fatigue or other physical abnormalities, and also inveighs against any sort of false subjectivism in the interpretation of mystical experiences in general. He insists with Hocking upon the "principle of alternation" of worship with work, and, as is evident, stresses even more than does Hocking the practical effects of "problem-solving" mysticism; its very name suggests its functional character. Thus, while his interpretation obviously has much in common with that of Hocking, he agrees with Macintosh that Hocking draws false inferences in his definition of the *object* of religious experience. His description of God in terms of "the Whole" rests upon a confusion of the "wholeness" of mystical experience with the character of its referent, an invalid psychologism, he says. Furthermore, Wieman believes that it is unempirical to describe the object of such experience in terms of "Other Mind", for reasons which we shall summarise below. Nor is the object to be construed as "supernatural" except in the sense that it may introduce the experient to a new pattern of experience and habit and hence to what for him is "another" world.[28] In short, Wieman like Macintosh remains strictly realistic in his analysis of religious experience and views any hypostatization of "the Whole" or the Absolute and the notion of an experience of such an entity as unempirical. At the same time, he seeks to make religious experience more objective than Macintosh's "right religious adjustment" and holds that it is rooted in sensory awareness.

In doing so he points out that the mystical experience described is not void of sensory content; while such content is undiscriminated, the experience itself is actually the richest of all in sensuous complexity.[29] In the complex of events involved in this type of religious experience there are necessarily *some* sensory elements. And,

> since God is that something which sustains human life he sustains the senses, he affects the senses. But anything that affects the senses is an object which may be perceived when men learn to note and interpret its sensuous effect. Hence God is an object to be perceived through sense experience.

It should be noted that Wieman hastens to add that he does *not* wish to imply that God is characterised by spatial magnitude or that he can be "handled" in any manner like other physical objects. Rather he means that there are "ways of apprehending" sense-experience which reveal that "factor" upon which maximum increase of value depends, and that "when this way of apprehending becomes established as a form of habitual reaction rendered accurate through experimental tests, we perceive God".[30] In other words, the mystical experience of God as described by Wieman is a "sense-experience" insofar as it involves "the *sense* of communion with the order of life . . . this appreciative consciousness that comes over us when we *sense* the growing organic order and community in which our little mechanism-preoccupied minds are embedded".[31]

Thus Wieman has claimed that God is an object of sense-perception for at least three ambiguous reasons: First, no experience is void of sensory content (though we may note that mystics have traditionally denied this with reference to their most crucial experiences!). Second, if God "sustains" life or is some process in the world, then he "affects" the senses through that which he "sustains". Third, we may say metaphorically that in some situations we seem to "sense" the order of life. Now we maintain that this last claim renders the term "sense" as vague as Macintosh's term "intuition", and that the other two arguments are equally unconvincing as proofs that God is an object of sense-perception in anything like the same manner as are tables and chairs, or other precisely delineated and controllable objects of macroscopic experience, though Wieman has at times maintained that such is the case. Though he has cited the works of H. H. Price and other logical empiricists as having been influential in the formulation of his views of perception, it seems clearly evident that what he has meant by "sense-perception" with reference to God is far different from what they mean by this term! And we have seen that in more recent statements of his theory of perception he himself would seem to question the cognitive significance if not the possibility of such states as "undiscriminated event", or "immediate awareness of the total passage of nature". He now recognizes the significant role of the defining concept in any type of perceptual experience and would thus seem to be forced to deny that "immediate experience", void of inferential guidance, is possible. Therefore it would seem that he must abandon or at least severely modify some of the arguments which he has used in support of the view that God is an object of sense-perception of the direct sort described in terms of "problem-solving mysticism". It would seem that one could hold that there is at least a minimum of sensory content in all perception, as well as believe that God is somehow related to the world of sense-perception, without maintaining that God himself is a sense-datum. It surely does not follow from a conception of God as that which "sustains" certain natural processes and thus indirectly "affects" the senses that God is thus one sense-object among others in the sensory manifold.[32] Rather it seems that the holding of such a view must be bound up, as suggested, with the interests of religious apologetic, and that it involves a loose usage of terms which results in unnecessary ambiguity.

But we have indicated that Wieman's view of religious perception is bound up, not only with his analysis of perception in general and with "problem-solving mysticism" as definitive religious experience, but also with his general theory of value and the idea of God as primarily a value-object. A brief summary of his value-theory is thus in order at this point, since it may shed further light on his general religious empiricism. For he, like Macintosh, holds that values are perceptible facts and that they constitute the primary data for religious inquiry, since religion is concerned with loyalty to supreme value.[33] Any distinction between value and fact in this realm is confusing, he says:

> We believe a great deal of confusion in religious thought may go back to the [assumption] that values are not facts. If value is a fact, just as truly anything else, then many of the difficulties in the search for God would fade away as dreams. If values are in nature and are facts, God can be found as readily and naturally as other persistent and pervasive realities.[34]

In what sense, then, are values perceptible facts? He has defined value as "that connection between enjoyable activities by which they support one another, enhance one another, and, at a higher level, mean one another".[35] Value, it should be noted, is order and connection and not mere enjoyment; increase in value means increase of interconnections between enjoyable activities. Enjoyments, in other words, are the "raw material" of value; values are connections which are found to be efficacious in promoting a wider connection between mutually enhancing enjoyments, and subjective immediate enjoyments must be derived from apprehensions of this broader function of value. Value-*judgments*, in other words, "enstate" values. Value itself is that connection between activities "which makes them truly enjoyable". The use of the term "appreci*able*" in the description of value-activity is necessary for objectivity and to guard against simple hedonism.[36]

Wieman's indebtedness to Dewey in this theory is gratefully recognized by him; indeed, he has said that "it is a doctrine which we believe is not essentially different from his [Dewey's] view".[37] His refusal to separate values from nature is clearly in line with Dewey's position. And this refusal to make a sharp ontological distinction between the realms of value and of fact leads him also to reject the preferential treatment given to "ideals" in metaphysics by Brightman and other ethical idealists. If one reifies conceptual ideals, he says, then all concepts must share this status indiscriminately, and the resulting chaos can only be overcome through a further appeal to experience; ideals, in other words, are functional guides in the interpretation of experience but are not "transcendental".[38]

But to infer from this analysis that values are perceptible facts involves a certain ambiguity which seems unwarranted. Wieman seems to mean that values understood as *"norms"* are perceptible like trees and stones, are given elements of gross experience. This meaning of value as normative is especially clear in his concept of God, to which we turn shortly. But it should be noted that what he actually points to as perceptually factual in gross experience is, not norms or value-*judgments* which "enstate" value, but rather the *"raw-material"* of such judgments, namely certain enjoyments and sufferings, or affective qualities, and "the fact" that these ordinarily occur in certain clusters or interconnections. As Dewey has pointed out, it is "a fact" that gross experience is characterised by pleasurable and painful qualities, that preferences as well as confrontations are characteristic of all experience. To say "this is pleasing" is a statement of *fact,* and as such is beyond criticism other than that derivable from factual analysis, in this case psychological. But, continues Dewey, there is a genuine difference between the "mere report of an already existent fact", (using "fact" in this context to refer to "value" as pleasure-pain or choice), and "judgment as to the importance and need of bringing a fact into existence. The latter is a genuine practical judgement, and marks the only type of judgement that has to do with the direction of action".[39] Such practical or value-judgments involve values understood as *norms,* and these in turn are constructed *on the basis of* an empirical analysis of affections or choices. They are objects of inference—concepts to be tested, not themselves percepts in the sense that macroscopic quantitative and qualitative elements in experience are. Of course, one may hold that "it *is* 'a fact' " that in human experience such norms are used in certain ways; this much may be gained from empirical observation, along with the "fact" that affective qualities in experience are "given" and are linked in certain ways to one another. But to say that the *norms* themselves are perceptually or factually given in the same sense in which "enjoyments" are is to use the term "fact" ambiguously. It is, in brief, a counterpart of Wieman's broad use of the term "perception" and affords a perceptual or "factual" basis for religious empiricism only through a questionable use of language. Further implications of this theory of value will be seen in the subsequent analysis of his concept of "supreme value" or God.

We turn now to examine Wieman's conception of the empirical method in terms of which religious perceptions are to be verified and interpreted. For his empiricism seems, in the last analysis, to be primarily methodological in import. Though he, like Macintosh, believes that God may be perceived in certain definite ways, he has insisted more emphatically than has Macintosh upon an exclusive and consistent employment of empirical method in all phases of religious philosophy. It is the function of a clearly defined method of approach to prepare one for valid religious experience as well as to test the worthiness of such experience when it occurs, and no speculative superstructure should be established on the basis of empirical foundations. Furthermore, it is the function of empirical method in the life of devotion itself to bring authentic religious insights to practical fruition. Thus "the question of method . . . is fundamental. . . . Only as we settle this question can we hope to settle any other, for it underlies every other".[40]

What, then, is his conception of the appropriate method for the verification of religious as well as all other types of perception? Despite the fact that this problem is a crucial importance for him, it seems that he is far from clear in his answer to this question, and that upon occasion he has qualified the methodological emphasis itself. In many of his writings, especially the earlier ones, he calls the universal method of verification "scientific method", claiming that science is (by definition) "that method by which truth and error are discriminated and knowledge verified".[41] In other words, scientific method is "simply the method of knowing. . . . All knowledge is scientific except insofar as it has not developed a method for discriminating the false and the true".[42]

However, he elsewhere gives more content to the term "scientific method" than that afforded by the view that knowledge is *scientia* in the broad sense of that term. More specifically, it is the purpose of science to "formulate definite concepts of those features of experience which can be certainly predicted, accurately calculated, and experimentally treated in imagination". Because of the rigor of this goal only the simplest data of experience have as yet been selected for scientific investigation, but all are in principle open to it.[43] Such method is not exclusively either "empirical" or "rational" if these terms are used, as they have been traditionally, to imply inductive and deductive emphases. (Cf. Macintosh's stress on the *inductive* character of empirical method.) It is, rather, the broad "method of sensory observation, experimental behavior, and rational inference, these three working together." Its progressive accuracy as much upon more rigorous and purer rational inference as upon more selective and refined observation or more completely controlled experiment.[44] And, since its aim is the prediction and control of the flux of events, the results of its application are always tentative; it can never yield absolute assurance, though it offers the most justified approach to certain knowledge which man has yet envisioned.[45]

This description of scientific method seems clear enough and is evidently a reasonably faithful account of the familiar method which is the working tool of the exact natural sciences. Furthermore, we should maintain that it is this method as so understood which, being generally accepted as the method of empirical sciences, should logically be meant and utilized when one speaks of empirical philosophy of religion. A consistent employment of such method might limit the function of such an enterprise in a manner which most of the empirical philosophers whom we have studied would not accept, and might be productive of certain difficulties in its own right. But at least the undertaking would be intelligible, would have clearly defined goals and motives, and would be generally free from ambiguity as to purpose and technique.

But we have noted that the other empirical philosophers whom we have studied have insisted upon a modification or supplementation of this method of natural science in the development of theological "hypotheses" and doctrines. And, though Wieman insists more strongly than do the rest upon its importance, in practice the method which he uses for the verification and apprehension of religious truth embodies many significant modifications of strictly scientific method. "Scientific method as applied to religion", he says, involves not only the working procedure of the exact sciences but also the more general techniques of "intelligence" or "common-sense", and includes among its data such items as the visions of saints and "intuitions of love".[46] Elsewhere he says that he hesitates to call the method of religious verification "scientific" at all, because he does *not* have in mind simply the technique of sciences like physics and chemistry; that he would call it "rational" method if this did not connote mere speculation with no experiential reference; and that he hesitates to call it "experimental" because he does *not* wish to imply that strictly scientific techniques may be employed.[47]

Verification of religious hypotheses cannot follow "any of the techniques of the special sciences", he says; "religion . . . so far as we can see at present, cannot make use of scientific method in the strict and narrow sense".[48] The religious datum is too complex for such a procedure; furthermore, an unrestricted application of such method would tend to "dry up" the all-important source of creative religious insight experienced in "problem-solving mysticism". Rather he holds, with Hocking, that mystical experience is the parent of scientific endeavor, and that it is important that such experience continue to furnish its unexplored and trans-scientific data if science is to retain its dynamic impetus and moral direction.[49] Furthermore, scientific method in the "narrow" sense of the term is unsuited to become the normative feature of religious insight because scientific beliefs are necessarily "tentative, merely intellectual devices", whereas religious belief must include elements of certainty and final decision. "Thus this [scientific] method cannot be a saving faith".[50]

We have mentioned these qualifying statements in some detail because it seems to us that they are of considerable significance for our study. Though Wieman, more than any of the other empirical theologians whose systems we have reviewed, insists upon the primacy of experimental method, it is clear that he is aware of and in agreement with many of the criticisms which have been directed against the view that the method of exact science may afford the best instrument for the formulation of religious faith. Many such criticisms have been directed against his own position, and the statements above serve to indicate that these criticisms spring from a misunderstanding of his intentions, or at least that in some of his writings he has significantly qualified the broad statements made in others. However, we are compelled to believe that a certain ambiguity and imprecision on his part are as much responsible for these criticisms as is the carelessness of his readers. In view of the importance which he places upon method in philosophy, it is unfortunate that he at times chooses the term "scientific" to indicate the type of approach to religious problems which he has in mind, since for many readers this phrase has many connotations which he himself finds inappropriate for religious inquiry. Whether the method which he does employ is enough like the more narrowly scientific to retain many of these same difficulties, is the question to which we now turn.

The broader method which he feels is appropriate to religious investigation he has called "the experimental method of common sense". It involves the *living out* of the implications of religious beliefs with an awareness of what one is doing, as opposed to any blind espousal of "an admixture of ideas from other sources". The "experiment" differs from ordinary laboratory experiments in that it is the most "hazardous" of all, involving the total commitment of life.[51] This "method of intelligence" (Dewey) is like the narrower scientific method in that it involves the formulation of a working hypothesis as the result of observations of human experience, ascertaining the conditions under which the course of action suggested in the hypothesis may be followed most successfully, the actual performance of appropriate acts and observation of the results, and the development by logical inference of resultant concepts and predictions of future experience.[52] Scientific method in the narrower sense, he says, is really a "refinement" of this broader "method of intelligence".

And in the "method of intelligence" or experimental method as applied to religious problems the crucial step is the first one, that is, the formulation of the hypothesis to be "tested". This may occur through "intuition", the character of which is influenced by tradition and "authority". Furthermore, since religion involves not simply the "understanding" of its object for purposes of exploitation and control—indeed does not seek to exhaust the mystery of its object at all—but rather includes attitudes of awe, adoration, and appreciation and leads to total commitment of self to that "object" held to be supremely worthful; therefore the narrower method of science with its aim at prediction and control would "cramp and distort" religion "out of all recognition".[53] Therefore in the "method of intelligence" as applied to religion, strictly scientific method is supplemented with what Wieman calls "philosophic method". Through the latter, that reality towards which scientific method (used broadly) is to be directed is more carefully delineated, by means of "a process of dialectical inquiry" which seeks to clarify those "deepest concepts and meanings which underly everyday meanings".

Religion, therefore, may become "scientific" only in the sense that it may become in some respects experimental; that is, it may develop techniques whereby it is possible to predict certain consequences as following empirically upon the adoption of certain religious hypotheses; it may "scientifically" relate alternative hypotheses to "naive experience" as a living whole.[54] But the formulation and "grasping" of a religious hypothesis itself and, it would seem, the final choice among hypotheses *after* the various experiential consequences have been objectively demonstrated, granting that this is possible, would rest finally upon subjective decision, or "intuition", colored by tradition and perhaps by "authority". Furthermore, Wieman is careful to insist that in no case should the religious object itself in its fullness ever be identified without qualification with any hypothetical referent. Religious hypotheses "are at best meager abstractions and have their value not in determining the nature and richness of what is supremely worthful, but in guiding our practical conduct and directing our attentive appreciation in the right direction. The reality itself must be seen and felt to be infinitely richer than these beliefs." We know *that* God is "more than" the referent of any belief, but not *what* he is as thus "transcendental"; it is for this reason, indeed, that empirical beliefs about him are permanently open to criticism and reconstruction.[55]

In what sense, then, is the "method of intelligence" as used by Wieman scientifically empirical? It is clear that, although in some writings he has identified it with scientific method, he does so only by using the latter term very broadly, and that, in its application to religious problems, it differs significantly from the working procedure of exact sciences. Thus critics like Van Dusen seem justified in their claim that it would be less ambiguous if the broader and more general method of inquiry which Wieman actually employs were not called "scientific" at all.[56] Wieman, in replying to such suggestions, has indicated his willingness to abandon the term if usage actually justifies his doing so; yet he feels that since, in the experimental "method of intelligence", "observation, analysis, inference, and experiment" are actually used in some sense, there is at least some continuity between it and the methods of science. However, he has specifically said (see above) that in the case of religious thought the "observation" is extended to cover a multiplicity of phenomena involving complex patterns of human behavior and interpretation, and is subordinate in importance to the "intuition" of the hypothesis which follows.

Furthermore, the "analysis" and "inference" involved in religious inquiry are based upon value-judgments related in a complex way to the general cultural and specific religious background of the "analyst", and rest in part upon "flashes of insight" or "religious intuition", though these features are not emphasized by Wieman as explicitly as they are by Macintosh. And the "experiment" of faith is not tentative, objective, and primarily operational in motive; rather it involves total and final commitment of the believer, with deeply personal and subjective implications. Its aim is not more accurate control or exploitation of its "object", but rather deeper appreciation of and more complete devotion to it. Finally, in some manner the "object" of religious experiment is "seen" or "felt" to be infinitely richer and "other" than what the believer imagines it to be, somehow "transcending" any and all operational concepts which may be applied to it. In the case of other empirical sciences, however, the "objects" of inquiry are, by definition, simply the experimental referents of working hypotheses. Therefore it seems to us that insofar as "the method of intelligence" in religious faith *retains* any of the most significant features of scientific inquiry, it is, according to Wieman's own statements, inadequate to its function.

It seems, then, that Wieman has meant at least two significantly different things when he has advocated the employment of scientific or experimental method in religious philosophy. On the one hand, he has sought to describe in broad terms an experimental method of inquiry which has proved most fruitful in the establishment of scientific knowledge and in the development of total philosophies based upon such knowledge and employing something of the same sort of method in other fields of philosophical interest. On the other hand, he has described a method of religious *living* which is, at the most, only roughly analagous to such experimental method, "in spirit", but which involves certain antithetical features. Many living religions have perennially insisted upon the relevance of faith to action, of the "religious hypothesis" to total life-experience; they have insisted that "faith without works is dead", that "by their fruits ye shall know them". And, as we noted at the outset, periods of re-examination of traditional concepts aimed at relating them more significantly to living situations occur frequently in religious histories. It is this sort of emphasis, we believe, which lies at the heart of Wieman's emphasis on experimental method in "private religious living." But we believe that such an emphasis has been and can be made without insisting upon the employment of "scientific" or "experimental" method in the religious life; that, indeed, Wieman's own writings show that confusion and misunderstanding easily result when such terms are used in this connection.

But our analysis of his views of religious perception and religious method has pointed in various ways to the significance of his conception of God with respect to all the other features of his religious philosophy. The major problems which we have suggested in these analyses are epitomized, we believe, in this central doctrine. It may be that a basic ambiguity in this connection lies behind the other difficulties which we seem to find in his philosophy as a whole. We noted at the beginning of our discussion that he has attempted to formulate the idea of God in such a way that the question of his existence "becomes a dead issue". He believes that this is accomplished if God is defined as "the best there is and can be", or as that process or structure of processes "upon which human life is most dependent for its security, welfare, and increasing abundance".

But he has developed these "minimal" definitions in various ways. At one point in his intellectual pilgrimage he suggested that God as so defined is "that interaction between individuals, groups, and ages which generates and promotes the greatest mutuality of good . . . the richest possible body of shared experience", a definition suggesting Dewey's "religion of shared experience".[57] In another volume he speaks of God as "that interaction which sustains and magnifies personality . . . the process of progressive integration";[58] while in another place he undertook to defend Whitehead's view of God as "the principle of concretion".[59]

All of these definitions seem to point to God as a sustaining process or condition of value. But he has also spoken of God as *the* "supreme" value, as the *goal* of value-achievement. Thus he says that if a "good" is "any fulfillment of interest", then the "supreme good" must be "the fulfillment of the most inclusive interest . . . or the most inclusive system of interests".[60] The greatest *conceivable* "value", he says, would be "the organization of this cosmos into that sort of system where every activity in it would be sustained by every other, and each activity would have all the meaning of the total system". But, he adds, the greatest *conceivable* value is not the *supreme* value, because the supreme value must be related to actual as well as to conceivably possible goods—suggesting, again, Dewey's view of God as that which links the actual with the possible. "True values are in God and God is in nature", he writes; thus the supreme value or true ideal is "the best that can be made out of the totality of all being" through intelligent aspiration and work.[61]

The concept which most adequately embraces and expresses both actual achievement of value and the unlimited future possibilities of greater value-achievements, he has said, is the concept of growth. By "growth" is understood "not merely what is, nor merely what might be, but that kind of change which increases what is, so as to approximate what might be . . . the growth of meaning in the world". It is "creative synthesis . . . the union of diverse elements in such a way that the new relation transforms them into a whole that is very different from the mere sum of the original factors". Of course only "connective growth" constitutes value; "competitive" or "thwarting" growths are disvalues, and mere increment is not necessarily efficacious in the promotion of wider mutuality. The "supreme value", therefore, is the unlimited connective growth of value-connections; God is "the growth of meaning and value". In other words, "the" supreme value is the "value" of increasing values: the connective growth of connective growths.[62]

But we may ask at this point whether it is fruitful to speak of the increase of values as "a" value: whether devotion to value-producing activities may be said to be either "a" value in itself or devotion to "a" value. The types of "connections between enjoyable activities" which, according to Wieman's definition, constitute values, seem to be varied and, in many instances, conflicting and contradictory. And he himself has said that the notion of a condition in which all such conflicts are removed is only a "conceivable" ideal and not "the" supreme value. But if actual value-connections are plural and sometimes contradictory, by what criteria is one to determine which value-activities lead towards the achievement of the ideal? Is the notion of one process or structure embracing all value-processes which enhance other value-processes in such a way as to promote the growth of the whole itself more than an imaginative construct? Is there any conceivable sense in which one may "point" to "the" process which includes the enhancement of all others—indeed, is this "supreme value" one process or structure among others in any sense? It is difficult to conceive just what "the" connective growth of connective growths may signify. In brief, it seems that when Wieman speaks of "the" supreme value he employs highly figurative and imaginative language and is no longer speaking of a definitely structured and definable object, entity, or "process" at all. Even on his own terms it would seem that the only empirically evident data in this connection are *processes*, not "a" process.

But we have noted that Wieman defines God not simply in terms of the maximum achievement of value, analogous to an ideal of perfection, but also in terms of those natural conditions which underlie the achievement of value. God, in other words, in not simply the greatest possible value or the process by which such value is achieved; he is also the sum-total of all the natural *conditions* of such value-achievement. Thus in a recent article he says that "the value of God . . . is that of creative source . . . that peculiar sort which pertains to the creator of all created values. The value of God is the value of creativity". In this sense God seems to be the underlying "ground" or the "power" behind the creation of value. Indeed, Wieman says that such a conception "comes very close to that of dominant power". He says that this does not imply that God as so conceived is "the source of everything" but only of "what generates the appreciative mind of man and the appreciable world relative to such a mind". God is, in other words, "the generative source of all good . . . the creative source of all other value". It is in this sense that God is "absolute" and "transcendent". He is absolute in that no amount of "created" good can "add or subtract" from his value, since his is the value of creativity as such; he is transcendent in that the "end" of all creativity cannot be imagined, and the possibilities for creativity in any particular situation cannot be apprehended. He is absolute and transcendent since, as creator, he "gives to man all the intelligence and ability with which he turns against" him . . . "God's power is incomparable and incommensurable with that of man."[63]

But further questions are in order with respect to this view of God as creator. If he means to refer to the natural conditions which may be utilized in the achievement of value, then once again we must point out that empirically there is a *plurality* of such conditions, and the notion of "a" creative "source" is at most imaginative and figurative. Furthermore, if one is to use figurative language and refer to "a" source, it is not clear how one can distinguish between the "source" of "the appreciative mind of man and the appreciable world relative to such a mind" and "the creator of everything"—especially if one takes an organic view of nature, as Wieman has attempted to do. Are any natural processes *unrelated* to the "generation" of the mind of man and "the appreciable world related to it"? If one is to speak of "a source" in this connection then it would seem that this source might well be the "source" of all "reality", though Wieman would deny this, as we shall see when we turn to his treatment of the problem of evil. But perhaps the underlying ambiguity here is the shifting from "the process of creativity" to the idea of "the creator". We have already questioned the idea of "a" process of creativity, though there may be various "creative" processes, and we would maintain that to speak further of the "power" and "goodness" of "creativity" described as "a creator" leads only to greater confusion.

It is interesting to note, in this connection, that Dewey has pointed to some of these ambiguities in objecting to Wieman's claim that his idea of God is a faithful theistic formulation of the religious faith implicit in Dewey's own philosophy. Dewey states that, while he has suggested that the term "God" may have the functional significance of linking the actual with the ideal and that the achievement of imagined ideals involves the utilization of certain natural forces, the kind of theistic formulation which Wieman wishes to derive from this view might just as well result in a polytheism as in a monotheism. There is a plurality of ideals to be envisioned and there is a plurality of natural forces involved in their achievement. Furthermore, the "unification" of ideals and implementing forces is simply the work of human imagination. The human community is the matrix in which ideals and aspirations are evolved, and such a community, set in the total framework of nature, should not be reified and worshipped. And, since nature embraces both "good" and "bad" human impulses and ideals, it is his opinion that Wieman has "fallen into a double confusion".[64]

Now it seems to us that, from a more consistently empirical point of view, Dewey's criticisms are justified; indeed, it seems that he has pointed clearly to the chief sources of difficulty in Wieman's total view. When Wieman speaks of God there seem to be at least three different meanings. He seems to mean the ideal of perfection or of the achievement of maximum value; the human and social processes which aim at the achievement of value; and the natural forces underlying or utilized in these processes. He does not realize that these three meanings may be viewed as constituting a unity (or a Trinity!) only in a highly imaginative and figurative sense, a sense appropriate to the life of faith and devotion, perhaps, but not to a religious philosophy which would be consistently empirical. We believe that it is his failure to be consistently empirical in this connection which is largely responsible for the confusions which we have found in his views of religious perception and method. When he has said that God may be "perceived" he has meant that in a certain kind of mystical experience there may be a "sense" of communion with life and a vision of ideal possibilities, *or* that we may perceive certain natural processes which are involved in value-achievement. When he speaks of scientific method in religion he means that men may "believe" in visions of ideal possibilities conceived as "hypotheses" and devote themselves intelligently to concrete activities, *or* that experimental method may be employed in gaining a greater knowledge of and mastery over nature in the service of ideal ends. In each case there seems to be unempirical imprecision as to just which meaning is intended in specific contexts.

Putting the matter in terms of the traditional theistic arguments, it may be said that Wieman is really employing a form of the ontological argument modified by a certain admixture of the teleological in his view of God. We have seen that he would make the question of "proof" of God's existence irrelevant *by definition,* in terms of "the best there is or can be" or "that upon which life depends for enhancement and support", and so on. We have also noted the major role played in his later views of religious perception by the definitive *concept* of deity. But this raises the perennial question whether the existence of anything can be "proved" by definition, by the refinement of a concept, and especially whether the existence of such a being (or "process") as "the best there is" can be so proved, particularly in view of the empirical difficulties suggested above. Calhoun, in criticising Wieman's views, has argued that his notion of God as supreme value is arrived at by a process similar to that involved in the Thomistic argument *ex gradibus,* inferring from the existence of particular goods the notion of a supreme good and assuming that such a good must necessarily exist. Such a procedure, as he points out, is ultimately Platonic and is hardly compatible with the empirical tradition in which Wieman would place it. And, while Wieman explicitly attempts to avoid this kind of formulation, we are inclined to agree with Calhoun that it is implicit in his view. Or, on the other hand, if he seriously means to identify the object of faith with an existent good or "process", then he must abandon his strictures against bondage to particulars and his recent emphases upon the transcendence of God.

In brief, it seems fair to say that Wieman's "empirical" view of God is derived primarily from his conceptual formulation of the "category for deity" rather than from an empirical survey of human experience, religious or otherwise, or from a consistent application of experimental method in the interpretation of such experience. Once God has been defined it may be said that if such a being or process exists he or it would have certain characteristics; but, as Calhoun has put it, in passing from hypothetical to assertoric judgment "we abandon logical rigor for the empirical assertion pervaded by analogical assumptions of the type: *tout comme ici*".[65] That Wieman conceives the original choice of concept for deity to be definitive in religious inquiry is evident from the foregoing analysis, and from his statement that

if one analyses the concept of the reality under consideration until he finds what is essential he has a different concept, and then, if by direct observation one discovers the reality in question to be in existence, one can, following this, make the sweeping generalization that this reality always and everywhere has this essential nature. . . .[66]

And we have raised several questions about the possibility of "discovering the reality under consideration" in religious inquiry as he defines it to be "in existence", "by direct observation".[67]

In developing further implications of his idea of God, Wieman seems to limit himself more rigorously to inferences derivable from the empirical subject-matter as conceived by him than do others who have figured in our study. Since he is not restricted in his view of the nature of experience as is Brightman, and since he disavows the frankly speculative superstructure which Macintosh rears on the foundation of his "empirical" theology, he cannot hold that God is primarily mental or personal in character. Personality, he points out, is inconceivable apart from a society of persons, with their mutual interaction among themselves and with the rest of nature; since God is the order of the existence and possibility of value he must underlie and include such interpersonal relations. And since no personality could even in principle be "perfect" in an imperfect society such as the only one open to empirical observations, there is further reason for holding that the idea of God as personal is "self-contradictory". It is true that God responds to personal adjustments in a "personal" manner, and that his nature must be so conceived that it accounts for the existence of personality; that, in brief, God is not *impersonal*. Therefore Wieman uses the personal pronoun in referring to God, being at the same time conscious of its inadequacy.[68]

For similar reasons he cannot conceive of God as "mind". Mind and personality are "summit characters" in nature, but they are not universal features of nature as are process and interaction. If God "has a summit" it must be "higher" than mind or personality; "they are the highest expressions of the kind of beings that display them . . . [but] I hold that God towers in unique majesty above the little hills which we call minds and personalities". God is the order of matter and the source of those interactions which constitute the structures of life and mind, yet he is not identical with nature as a whole or with any specific "level" thereof; he is "beyond" each of these levels as they are "beyond" each other. "God is more than we can think, but his working is manifest and inescapable".[69] Of course we have already questioned the empirical basis for the assertion of this type of transcendence; nevertheless, the *negative* aspect of the doctrine, resting as it does upon a broader view of the empirical "subject-matter", seems more consistent than the more definite views of other empirical philosophers.

A further consequence of Wieman's view of God as growth of meaning and value is his position on the "problem of evil" which is of such significance for Brightman and others. From a consistently empirical point of view, he holds, this is really a false problem; it arises only when one departs from the empirical evidence for God as "the good", or the chief factor for good in nature, and begins to speculate about God as also somehow the creator of all existence. That is, one must either deny the reality of evil, which is clearly unempirical, or give up the idea of God as Creator of all, or as the Whole or Absolute, even if the latter be conceived as a Supreme Person. Brightman's idea of a finite deity only reformulates the false problem, which as stated is truly "insoluble". The more empirical problem is to define the actual nature and scope of evil, and not to indulge in unempirical speculation as to its "origin". Good and evil are facts, and are bound up with "positive" and "negative" activities, the one enhancing and the other thwarting life; evil, in other words, exists only as a parasite; its ultimate triumph would mean annihilation. Though there can be no empirical certainty of the eventual "triumph" of good, it does seem to be empirically true that natural and human histories are characterized by increases in integration.[70] Thus Wieman, like Boodin, finds an ultimate dualism more empirical than either a monistic idealism which would deny the existence of evil, a quasi-monistic idealism which would seem to equivocate the issue, or a speculative attempt to "solve" the problem in terms of a morally-controlled world and the "saving" effect of a certain type of ethico-religious experience.

Of course many empiricists would insist upon a stricter pluralism of goods and bads relative to particular contexts and goals; it would seem that the empirical data consist solely of such elements in experience, so that any attempt to hypostatize such notions as "the good" and "the evil" runs beyond the bounds of strictly empirical analysis. And, while a dualism of this type avoids some of the more obvious speculative problems of ethical and metaphysical monism, it is beset with certain difficulties of its own—particularly when it is bound up with an idea of God such as Wieman's, which seems actually to include some notion of God as ground of *all* reality, despite his protestations to the contrary. Or, even if it be granted that God is simply the "source" of good, then, if one is to speak of "sources" in this manner, there is the additional question of the "source" of evil, and of the relation of the two "sources" to each other and to nature as a whole. It does not seem that the problem can be avoided at this level, either by describing religious devotion solely in terms of devotion to "the good", or by rendering evil "parasitic" by definition, as Wieman wishes to do.

However, our survey of Wieman's system has revealed that in many respects he seems to be more consistently empirical than any of the other philosophers who have figured in our study. In his view of experience and nature he seems to avoid the restrictive subjectivism and absolutism which characterises, at least to some extent, the systems of the three idealists whom we have studied. He is aware of some of the difficulties involved in any simple appeal to a particular kind of religious experience in the formulation of a religious philosophy, and he would avoid any speculative superstructure of "reasonable" over-beliefs beyond what seems to him to be the empirical evidence in the formulation of theological doctrines, differing in these respects from Macintosh. Nevertheless, we have sought to point out what seem to be major difficulties in his own view. We turn now to a critical summary of what seem to be the outstanding trends and problems in the general movement of thought illustrated by our five philosophers, following which we shall suggest some directions which a more consistent and less ambiguous "association of empiricism with religion" might take.

4

CONCLUSION

W_E suggested at the outset that, while the rise of various movements claiming to be "empirical" constitutes a most significant trend in recent philosophical thought, there is widespread disagreement as to just what the terms "empirical" and "empiricism" should mean. In actual practice, we said, at least three broad connotations seem to be implied. To be "empirical" in the approach to philosophical problems may mean simply to be "realistic" or "tough-minded": to take full account of all the relevant data and to blink none of the significant "facts", to ask for no easy solution for complex problems and to demand no certainty or assurance which would involve an "escape" from "reality". Or empiricism may be associated primarily with an "appeal to experience" in the establishment and defense of philosophical doctrines, a deference to the "given", whether "experience" be conceived as consisting essentially of sense-data, or whether it be construed more liberally. Again, empiricism may be viewed as primarily methodological in import, signifying a particular type of inquiry, usually with an emphasis upon "a posteriori" hypothesis and induction as over against rationalistic *schema* and logical or metaphysical "a-prioris".

The five philosophies of religion examined in this study may be said to be empirical to some degree in each of these three senses. We have found that each of our philosophers seeks to take a broadly "realistic" attitude towards the problems of religion. Each would base his religious views upon "the facts of experience", either experience in general or some form of religious experience in particular. And each would establish his conclusions through an appeal to some form of empirical method.

Indications of the "realistic" or tough-minded approach are seen in an explicit abandonment, even on the part of the idealists, of the older rationalistic ideal of absolute certainty or "finished" truth which implies a static and eternally valid blueprint of reality in its "ultimate" nature. The full implications of this break with the absolutistic ideal are perhaps seen less clearly by Hocking and Brightman than by Boodin, Macintosh, and Wieman, but it is reflected to some extent in the systems of all five thinkers. Thus Hocking would take account of the contingency and open-ness implied in an experimental or scientific view of the world, while in-sisting at the same time upon the relevance of some intuition of certainty and some notion of "the Whole". Brightman also feels that a particular view of "the Whole" is necessary for any "coherent" understanding of all the facts of experience, but he believes that in metaphysics as in other areas of thought it is possible to have only "practical" certainty. Boodin finds the idea of a "cosmic context" suggested by the experimental procedures of the various sciences as such. Macintosh would claim certainty in his "empirical theology" only for those doctrines immediately implied in what he takes to be a scientifically valid type of religious experience, while he insists that reasonable "overbeliefs" are of a speculative and therefore less certain character. And Wieman would limit all metaphysical speculation to such evidence as is afforded by scientific inquiry, interpreted in a naturalistic framework.

Specific illustrations of the results of this "realistic" approach are seen in our philosophers' treatments of certain religious doctrines. The idea of God, for instance, is considerably different in most of these philosophies from what it is in traditional Christian dogmatic theologies or in those rationalistic and idealistic religious philosophies which identify God with a transcendent and timeless Absolute. Because the reality of time is taken seriously, God is viewed as "Creator" only in the temporal sense—that is, in terms of a continuous process of creativity. This means, too, that He is "eternal" only as One who endures through all time. Furthermore, he is not viewed as "transcendent" in the sense that this term has often been used in traditional theology. He is not conceived as a being existing "apart" from "the world", but rather as immanent in "the world", as one "factor" or "process" among others, or, in the case of the idealists, as One in Whom "the world" itself has intelligible being.

Because of these views of the relation of God to the world, and because of the general "realistic" desire to take seriously all of the "facts" relevant to ethical analysis, our philosophers also differ from traditional dogmatic theologians and absolutistic religious philosophers in their treatment of "the problem of evil". Hocking, it is true, holds that all evils are somehow "transmuted" in the absolute perspective, but he insists upon the reality and significance of moral conflict and struggle in temporal existence. Brightman goes further and holds that a genuinely empirical recognition of "surd evil" leads to a view of God as "finite" or limited, eternally strug-gling against a "Given". Boodin, in turn, finds a clear-cut cosmological and ethical dualism to be more consistent and to do greater justice to the "facts". Macintosh reverts to a more traditional view in maintaining that, if the world would be interpreted in light of the primary significance of a religio-ethical experience of salvation, then it may be held that ours is the best possible world for the spiritual education of man. His views on this subject, however, are admittedly more speculative than are the direct conclusions of his "empirical" theology. And Wieman would adopt a kind of dualism with respect to evil, maintaining that God is the source only of good and that the only real "problem of evil" is the problem of how to overcome specific evils through intelligent activity.

In brief, the "realistic" approach of our empirical philosophers to religious problems results in an abandonment of many emphases associated with "transcendentalism" in philosophy and theology. All are concerned to make their religious beliefs "experience-centered" and directly relevant to the readily observable facts of everyday living. They would fashion a vital religious philosophy which takes full account of the modern scientific outlook in general and the established results of the natural sciences in particular, a philosophy which is both intellectually respectable and dynamically effective in affording a satisfactory guide to understanding the problems of life. They would make explicit in terms suitable to the modern outlook what is "the meaning of God in human experience".

This suggests that they would all base their religious philosophies upon an "appeal to experience". In doing this they take, for the most part, a broader view of "experience in general" than have some traditional empiricists. In no case is their empiricism "sense-bound", though each is aware of the significance of sensory elements in experience, and Wieman at one time placed a primary emphasis upon these in his interpretation of experience as a whole. But Hocking is critical of traditional idealism for minimizing the importance if not denying the reality of affective and volitional elements in experience, while Brightman views the "datum-self" as an entity of rich complexity. Boodin would interpret experience even more liberally by refusing to exaggerate the importance of subjective elements as Hocking and Brightman, despite their broadened views, seem to do. Macintosh and Wieman, in turn, also insist upon the equal "reality" of both objective and subjective as well as of volitional and affective elements.

But there are certain differences in their "appeals to experience" for the establishment and defense of religious doctrines. Hocking finds a certain idea of God both implied in the analysis of natural and social experience and directly given in a particular sort of mystical religious communion. Brightman believes that the existence of a Cosmic Person is implied in epistemological analysis, in the most "coherent" interpretation of modern scientific knowledge, and in ethical and religious experience. Similarly, Boodin finds the existence of a world-spirit or cosmic context implied in various areas of inquiry and directly suggested by religious communion.

Macintosh, however, appeals primarily to one specific type of religious experience to prove the existence of a "divine value-producing factor", while Wieman combines a naturalistic interpretation of various types of experience with an emphasis upon "problem-solving" mysticism in the life of devotion in establishing his religious philosophy.

And in all cases there is an appeal to some kind of empirical method for the verification of the religious doctrines held by each. Hocking would combine the openness of experimentalism with a basic intuition of "the Whole" in an "empirical dialectic". Brightman would take a more "liberal" view of empirical method and include within it all the ways of the mind involved in inquiry, including certain emphases more usually associated with rationalism as well as those which are more clearly in accord with a more precisely experimental approach. Macintosh would interpret empirical method primarily in terms of induction, while Boodin and Wieman would employ an experimental method at least analogous to that of scientific inquiry, in which deductive and inductive elements are combined in an operational and functional approach.

These, then, are some of the major trends appearing in five recent attempts to "associate empiricism with religion". A broadly conceived "realistic" outlook which would take seriously all the relevant facts is expressed in an "appeal to experience" which, in turn, suggests certain "religious hypotheses" to be verified by empirical method.

But this brief summary indicates, as our exposition has revealed in greater detail, that these broad points of agreement and common emphasis among our philosophers entail at the same time considerable divergence of viewpoints concerning specific problems. Thus we are led to ask whether it is fruitful or significant to designate as "empirical" any view which in any sense claims to be "tough-minded", to be based upon the "facts of experience", and to employ an empirical method of inquiry. It may be said that no philosopher or theologian has ever claimed that his system is *not* based upon the "facts of experience" as he understands those facts, and thus it could be said that, if the term be used inclusively, all philosophies and theologies are in some sense "empirical". Furthermore, we have seen that our philosophers employ various methods of inquiry in establishing their positions, and that some of them fall into the "fallacy of the suppressed correlative" in their definitions of method. We have also seen that in each case there is a close correlation between views of experience and concepts of method. Which view, then, is "empirical"? Are there any clearly definable characteristics which could be associated with a more precise understanding of what "empiricism" means?

Fundamental to any empirical philosophy, we believe, is an ideally objective and inclusive view of experience. While it may be granted that what is "found" in experience is determined in part by some regulative view of "the whole", nevertheless the empiricist may strive to avoid any undue emphasis upon any one aspect of experience which would distort his view of the whole. The systems of Hocking and Brightman indicate the results for religious philosophy of an exaggerated emphasis upon subjective and cognitive apects of experience. Conceptions of experience in which primary significance is ascribed to cognitive experiencing or "conscious awareness" may lead to the metaphysical principle that all existence must somehow be related to the experiencing of some person or mind, finite or infinite. Hocking employs his "psychologism" as one aspect of his case for the existence of an Other Mind to make intelligible the human experience of other minds and of nature, while Brightman is led from the view that experience is essentially conscious awareness, that the immediately "given" in experience is the "datum-self", to the view that all reality exists "in, of, or for" persons. Boodin, Macintosh, and Wieman, who take a more liberal view of experience, are not led for these reasons to identify God with Cosmic Mind.

We believe that a broader view of experience is more empirical, that it is more faithful to the heterogeneous, complex, and ongoing affair which is man's life in nature. That process of "undergoings", of "enjoyments and sufferings" which is "nature articulate" is not exclusively "physical" or "psychical", "objective" or "subjective", "quantitative" or "qualitative", "individual" or "social", cognitive, affective, or volitional. Rather it is all of these, as it is "immediately had", and any exaggerated emphasis upon any of these elements is based upon a false abstraction from the living whole which easily results in a distorted view of the "subject-matter" of empirical philosophy. Such a philosophy, if it is to be distinctively different from others with respect to this basic question, must take full account of plurality and variety in the material which constitutes the basis for its inquiries.

This general view of experience has special implications for religious philosophy, and particularly for those philosophies which place special emphasis upon some form of religious experience. Such an emphasis quite often tends to minimize the role of the interpretive theory in terms of which the crucial religious experience is judged to be significant, as well as to overlook the limitations imposed by the particular cultural context in which such an experience has religious value. Thus we have found in Hocking's religious philosophy an emphasis upon a certain kind of mystical experience, the value of which is expressed by him partly in terms of his general epistemological and metaphysical viewpoints, while these are in turn open to criticisms of various kinds. It is significant to note that Wieman emphasizes what seems to be essentially the same sort of experience, but derives from it quite different conclusions. We have pointed out several difficulties inherent in any delineation and interpretation of mystical experience as such, suggesting that definitions and interpretations alike appear in such variety that any "empirical" grounding of a particular religious philosophy in one type seems highly questionable. Is the theory vindicated by the experience, or the experience by the theory? Are not experience and theory so intimately and subtly related as to render any defense of the one in terms of the other precarious?

This question is especially pertinent, we feel, in the case of idealistic interpretations of religious experience. While Brightman and Boodin do not stress the importance of narrowly defined types, they do find religious experience understood as "any experience in its relation to the whole of experience", or as experience of a Cosmic Spirit, to be highly significant. Brightman further utilizes the notion of a "coherent" interpretation of "the whole" in finding religious significance in value-experience interpreted dialectically, and in claiming theistic implications for the conclusions of natural science. We have claimed that he seems ambiguous with reference to the question whether the God thus implied is in any sense *an* "object" of *an* experience or not. Apparently he may be said to be such only if it is held that "objects" of speculation are objects of particular experiences, on the grounds that experience is synonymous with consciousness and that the rational is the real. And this, we have maintained, narrows the meaning of "experience" and makes any "empiricism" derived from it ambiguous. In any event, it seems clear that Brightman's "appeal to experience" in establishing his religious philosophy involves many questionable theoretical assumptions which would have to be made explicit if not abandoned in a more precisely empirical approach.

The same implicit assumption that any appeal to experience necessitates a definite view of "the whole" of experience is involvd in Boodin's metaphysical views, and these in turn are reflected in his descriptions of religious communion. Though he maintains that the latter is essentially indefinable, his poetic descriptions of "the music of the spheres", implying a 'cosmic score" for the "cosmic harmony", suggest that the character of the religious experience to which he points is uniquely colored by his contextualistic approach to reality. Here again a certain kind of experience is singled out and labelled "religious" at least partly because of specific theoretical assumptions subject to criticism in their own right.

But it is in Macintosh's empirical theology that we have found the fallacies of an appeal to religious experience most clearly indicated, and it is he who most clearly rests his case for "empirical theology" upon the normative validity of a specific kind of experience. The "critical realistic epistemological monism" in terms of which he claims perceptual status for "right religious adjustment" involves various technical difficulties, some of which we have sought to indicate. His frequent appeals to "intuition"—a term which he uses with considerable ambiguity—in the defense of some of his conclusions, are also open to criticism. We have called attention to further ambiguities in his use of the terms "adjustment" and "factor". And we believe that we have shown that the kind of experience which is for him of primary and normative religious significance is not self-vindicating, whether or not it be labelled "perception" through a Pickwickian use of this term, but is rather dependent for its significance and theological validity upon certain value-judgments or definitive assumptions which are mistakenly taken by Macintosh to be inferences drawn from the experience itself. Subjective predispositions suggested in Macintosh's religious biography seem to play a major role in his selection of a specific type of "religious adjustment" which is defined as the "right" one upon which to build an empirical theology. The meaning and significance of such experience are interpreted in terms of value-judgments which, in a particular religious tradition, are matters of "common-sense". These judgments must at least be implicit if the experience which he describes is even to be *had*, and the having of the experience, along with the personal and social consequences which follow from it, simply indicates certain behavioral implications of the value-judgments themselves. Calling such adjustment "right" and its consequences fruitful or valid is a matter of personal faith related to a specific religious tradition.

In other words, the validity of Macintosh's "empirical theology" seems to rest upon the validity of what he calls "normative" or "valuational" theology, rather than the reverse, as he claims. And the validity of his normative theology is bound up, at least in part, with certain emphases of liberal Protestantism, along with an appreciation of that type of "conversion" experience which is emphasized in his account of "personal religion". Such specifically conditioned experiences, we maintain, cannot in themselves substantiate or verify those theological doctrines which must be presupposed before they may be had. Surely experiences of this sort differ in many important respects from the public and objective type usually implied in scientific inquiry. The "experience" to which our empirical philosophers of religion point in defending their views is a much more highly selective and subjectively-conditioned affair than is the broader and more neutral material immediately apparent to the more impartial and open-minded empirical investigator.

This question of the relation of experience to theory and interpretive concept also has an important bearing upon Wieman's description of the object of religious perception in terms of naturalistic theism. Though he has not overtly stressed the significance of "problem-solving mysticism" in some of his more recent writings as much as he did in some earlier ones, we have suggested that recent modifications in his general theory of percep tion and in his view of the religious object are definitely related to certain emphases associated with such experience. His descriptions of the richly complex and essentially undifferentiated immediacy which is said to be apprehended therein, insofar as it is interpreted as the pregnant and dynamic source of fresh scientific insight and creative personal relationships, suggest many of the characteristics attributed by him to God as "creativity". On the other hand, recent statements of his theory of perception which stress the rôle of definitive concepts in all perceptual awareness may be interpreted as a further attempt to afford valid perceptual status for a specific kind of religious insight.

We may conclude, then, that our philosophers' "appeals to experience", whether to experiences of various types interpreted in terms of religious categories or to one specific type of experience declared to be "religious" in itself, are fraught with difficulties. In appealing to essentially the same type of experience Hocking finds Other Mind where Wieman finds "Creativity". Brightman's religious interpretation of the "whole" of experience leads him to posit a Cosmic Person where Boodin posits a Cosmic Spirit or context. And Macintosh, appealing to a different sort of experience, finds God to be empirically a divine value-producing factor operative in ethico-religious salvation. Divergent theories interpreting a variety of experiences yield divergent conclusions. Thus, instead of discovering "the meaning of God in human experience" we seem to discover the meanings of God in the personal experiences of five men of faith as interpreted in five suggestive and stimulating but conflicting philosophies.

Therefore we agree with Moore, Aubrey, and others whose conclusions on the matter we have previously cited that the appeal to religious experience in the formulation of a religious philosophy generates as many problems as it supposedly solves. Such experience usually refers to some authority beyond itself for its authentication. This may be the authority of "intuition", the authority of the religious object to which it refers as enhanced by a given tradition, the authority of its consequences for private and social living, or the more general and subtle "authority" of the religious and philosophical assumptions of the experient. The fact that there are varieties of religious experience and of interpretations thereof suggests that specific types may be singled out as normative only through more or less arbitrary decision. As Moore puts it, the term "religious experience" "has to a considerable degree outlived its usefulness. Its popularity has rested in large measure upon its vagueness and ambiguity".[1]

But we have noted that our philosophers' methods of inquiry are also closely bound up with their views of experience in general and religious experience in particular. Thus we have seen that Hocking would employ an "empirical dialectic" in which free and tentative scientific inquiry is undergirded by an underlying notion of "the whole" apprehended with religious force and certainty. Brightman does not qualify his designation of his methodology as "empirical", though it seems actually to be closely akin to Hocking's "empirical dialectic". Brightman himself acknowledges his indebtedness to Hegel for his understanding of the dialectical character of empirical method and he insists that this is the authentic method of "radical empiricism". But we have shown that his understanding of such method is based upon his identification of experience with conscious awareness and the assumption that the rational is the real. Induction and deduction, fact and inference, "a-priori" and "a-posteriori" notions are utilized indiscriminately; and a particular notion of the character of "the whole" which is said to make "coherent" the pluralistic and ongoing patterns of experience underlies the entire enterprise. We have suggested that this all-inclusive interpretation of empirical method clearly illustrates the "fallacy of the suppressed correlative". If the term "empirical method" is to have a clearly-defined and useful meaning it must signify one particular type of inquiry and not all possible types.

Boodin, we have seen, does employ a more precisely defined methodology, similar in many respects to the experimental approach of natural science. Indeed, we have suggested that his religious philosophy is really a kind of "theology of natural science". But we have also asked whether his notion of a "spirit of the whole" and his Platonic dualism in ethics and cosmology are not reflections of more rationalistic emphases. Macintosh would make a sharper distinction between the speculative and rationalistic and the "empirical" aspects of his theology. His conception of empirical method as utilized in the latter emphasizes primarily the role of induction. But we have seen that he interprets "induction" as applied to theology quite broadly and, we believe, ambiguously; he even suggests that all deduction is, in a certain sense, induction. Furthermore, the material open to inductive inquiry in his system consists of the data afforded by a particular kind of "religious adjustment", a rather limited kind of subject-matter, as we have suggested above. And in his description of this subject-matter as well as in his account of empirical method he makes frequent appeals to what he calls "intuition", a term which seems to mean various things in various contexts. It thus seems evident that the "empirical method" used by Macintosh is not the experimental method of science.

Wieman has taken the normative status of "scientific method" more seriously in the development of his religious philosophy than have any of the other thinkers whom we have studied. In some of his writings he describes such method in a manner which renders it broadly equivalent to the working techniques of experimental sciences. But when he turns to the description of "methods of private religious living" he speaks of a more broadly conceived "method of intelligence", in which "scientific method" is supplemented by "philosophical method". At the same time he points out certain difficulties inherent in the employment of a strictly scientific outlook in the life of devotion. But we believe that these distinctions are not always explicit in his general descriptions of methodology as related to religious philosophy, and that confusion results from his failure to keep the distinctions clear. His conception of God as related to nature and to religious experience illustrates this underlying ambiguity.

This raises again the question as to just what the relation of "empirical method" to "scientific method" should be. Should these terms be viewed as essentially synonymous, do they indicate certain common emphases, or are they unrelated? The answer to such a question is of course arbitrary to a certain extent, and usage in such a case may be conventional. But attention to historical developments and a desire for maximum precision in philosophical discussion have led to more definite and hence more fruitful conceptions of empirical method than those which appear in our study. Dewey, whose "Empirical Survey of Empiricisms" we found useful at the outset in gaining some measure of historical orientation, has been particularly interested in developing an unambiguous understanding of what should be implied in a modern use of empirical method. It is evident that the increasing influence of empirical method in all branches of philosophy is definitely related to the rise of natural science and the successful employment of scientific inquiry in various areas of investigation. And we believe that a central motive underlying various attempts to develop "empirical" philosophies of religion has been a desire on the part of the philosophers to make certain religious beliefs "scientifically" justifiable and respectable. Whether this desire is misplaced from the standpoint of apologetics is a question to which we shall give further attention below.

In any case, we agree with Dewey that, in the light of historical developments and in the interests of clarity in philosophical discussion, empirical method like scientific method should be conceived as being primarily experimental. Its aim as thus conceived would be so to relate carefully selected and clearly defined segments of past and present experience that fruitful observations might be made concerning the patterns which similar configurations of experience would probably follow in the future. Thus "understanding" a given section of experience would mean indicating its functional relationship to other sections in specific contexts. In such "understanding" the locus of verification would be future, and judgments would always involve a certain amount of risk, making them open and tentative. Time, contingency, and novelty, the "ongoingness" and "unfinished" character of experience, as well as plurality and variety in ends, objects, and subject-matters would be taken seriously. Through such inquiry broader familiarity with progressively wider areas of experience would be gained, and understanding of particular areas would thus be enriched. Such method might be more exactly labelled "hypothetico-inductive", the second term of the definition indicating the major emphasis in its logical theory and the first term indicating the selective, tentative, and future reference of its accomplished operations. A more general emphasis in Dewey's understanding of this form of inquiry is upon the necessity for tracing back to "primary experience, in all its heterogeneity and fullness", any refined and technical abstraction made for specifically defined purposes in specialized types of inquiry. In other words, the final locus of all verification should be public, objective, and familiar.[2]

Now we have suggested that this latter emphasis is apparent in the philosophies examined in this study. Our philosophers, as representatives of the "liberal" tradition in Protestantism, have been concerned to state in terminology meaningful for the modern mind what is the "meaning of God in human experience". One of their aims is to make the life of devotion and its guiding concepts "experience-centered", and to this end they seek to ground their systems in what they take to be publicly available and semi-familiar experiences like "right religious adjustment" and "problem-solving mysticism". They would give new significance to traditional theological terms by pointing to specific "happenings" in the world, experiences which are, they believe, publicly available and valid as interpreted in terms of modern science and metaphysics. Insofar as their aim has been fulfilled our philosophers have made a constructive and positive contribution to the understanding and enrichment of the religious life.

But we have questioned the universality and objectivity of some of the experiences emphasized, and we have further indicated the extent to which the methods of investigation employed go beyond the "hypothetico-inductive" type of inquiry outlined above. Hocking maintains that such inquiry must itself rest upon certain commitments of a religious nature; Brightman broadens it into a general search for "coherence"; Boodin gives poetic expression to what he takes to be its speculative framework; Macintosh makes "induction" all-inclusive; and Wieman speaks more broadly in terms of a "philosophic method of intelligence". Thus our philosophers seem to be concerned, not merely with the employment in religious philosophy of empirical method as more precisely defined, but with what they take to be certain religious presuppositions of its employment in any area of thought. Dewey himself, of course, has suggested that an empirical analysis of the values normative in a liberal and democratic culture might lead to a religious devotion to scientific techniques for the achievement of ideal ends as the basic item in a "common faith".[3]

But here the emphasis is upon religious devotion to empirical method rather than upon the employment of empirical method in the investigation or practice of religious devotion. Indeed, it seems questionable whether empirical method as more precisely defined is appropriate to or compatible with certain features of some types of religious devotion, if, as we suggested earlier, "intimacy and ultimacy are the hallmarks of religion". Empirical method interpreted as being primarily experimental would aim at an objectivity and tentativeness quite different from those attitudes of personal commitment and trust which characterize certain types of religious decision and faith. Thus we have questioned Macintosh's claims that "experiments" in "religious adjustment" are basically similar in character to scientific experiments and that the "certainty" of scientific knowledge is similar to the "intuitive" certainty which, according to him, characterizes religious knowledge. We have also noted Wieman's recognition of the total and "ultimate" character of religious commitment as contrasted with other "experiments" involved in practicing the "method of intelligence", though we have suggested also that full implications of this distinction seem to be blurred in some of Wieman's writings. There is surely a fundamental difference between scientific experiment which aims at "adjustments" of man with environment in the interest of progressively stable human control over or exploitation of nature and that type of religious "adjustment" in which the believer seeks to become the increasingly pliable *object* of divine control.

However, experimentally empirical method could be employed in the investigation of religious beliefs and practices. Such investigation could also be clearly empirical in its view of its subject-matter, treating as objectively as possible many different kinds of religious phenomena. Thus James, whose remarks about the "association of empiricism with religion" we quoted at the outset, made a monumental contribution to the study of religion in his investigation of "the varieties of religious experience". It was at the conclusion of this study that he suggested further that "if (religious philosophy) will abandon metaphysics and deduction for criticism and induction, and frankly transform herself from theology into a science of religions, she can make herself enormously useful."[4] We should add that such a "science" of religions, if it were to be more thoroughly empirical, would have to take account of institutional and social religious practices as well as of types of religious *consciousness*.[5]

Furthermore, James went on to suggest that such a "science" of religions might have more than a primarily analytical or descriptive function. "The spontaneous intellect of man", he wrote, "always defines the divine which it feels in ways which harmonize with its temporary intellectual prepossessions. Philosophy can by comparison eliminate the local and accidental from these definitions . . . can also eliminate doctrines now know to be scientifically absurd or incongruous . . . [and] leave a residuum of conceptions that are at least possible. . . . As a result, she can offer mediation between different believers, and help to bring about consensus of opinion."[6] But this task, it seems, would take the investigator beyond what may be more properly called a "science" of religions into that more normative discipline usually called "philosophy of religion". It is this latter type of inquiry with which the philosophers of our study are primarily concerned. And our study has revealed that these five representative attempts to construct normative but "empirical" religious philosophies or "natural theologies" involve divergent methodological assumptions, interpretive *schema,* and personal religious convictions, implicit and explicit, which are the presuppositions rather than the results of their "empirical" inquiries. Thus it seems that, in religious philosophy of this type as well as in other normative philosophical disciplines, what the "empirical" thinker "finds" is largely colored by the basic assumptions with which he begins his "search". Or, to put the matter in theological terms, it seems that the "natural" theologian's reflections upon "general revelation" are necessarily guided by his attitude towards certain central convictions or "special revelation" which constitutes the subject-matter of a "revealed theology".

This reflection leads us into the complex and too often mooted question of the relation of philosophy of religion to theology, "natural" and "revealed". It is of course impossible within the scope of this study to enter into the question in any detail, but it is our belief that a general re-examination of the issue is a necessary task for contemporary philosophers and theologians. A brief suggestion of some of the issues involved and of some alternative viewpoints may be pertinent here, since our study of five philosophers of religion who have attempted in various ways to be more "empirical" in their approach to the traditional problems has revealed, we believe, certain underlying ambiguities concerning this fundamental question.

The distinction between philosophy of religion and theology has been made in various ways. Some thinkers would make universality as contrasted with particularity of religious belief the basis for distinction. Thus theology would be concerned to give a connected and "reasonable" account of dogmas implied in a specific type of religious faith, as "the science of faith", while philosophy of religion would be concerned to discriminate certain basic views common to all faiths, if there be such, and to delineate the nature of and basis for conflicting dogmas. This distinction we believe to be most fruitful. If it were observed there would be no question of philosophy's furnishing a "world-faith" in the religious sense, though its criticisms might illuminate some of the problems associated with this issue. A clearer distinction would be made between philosophy and religion,

though philosophical views might be held with religious fervor, while religious beliefs would surely have philosophical implications. In any event,
an empirical "science" of religion would have a definitely defined function
within such a scheme. It would be in part the function which James seems
to have envisaged for a "science of religions", though we believe that it
would be unempirical to attempt in such an enterprise to "eliminate the
local and the accidental", "historic incrustations", and so on, since these
seem empirically to be integral elements in the life of faith. Such a study
would certainly not "become the champion of one" religious faith or "hypothesis", "distinguishing between what is innocent over-belief and symbolism in the expression of it, and what is to be literally taken", in order
to offer "mediation between different believers".[7]

We shall have more to say about the role of symbolism and "historic
incrustations" in a moment. First we would suggest that what seems to be
partly implied in James' remarks is a different kind of relation beween religious philosophy and theology. In this view there seems to be an implica-
tion that only what has traditionally been called "natural theology" is any
longer intellectually respectable and religiously valid, that theologies must
be finally interpreted in a universal philosophy of religion which may or
may not have more in common with one of the many traditional theologies
of the world than with others. And this view, in turn, must be further distinguished from a third, in which "philosophy of religion" or "natural
theology" is looked upon as that enterprise which deals with those items
of belief in a specific faith which can be established and defended apart
from specific personal commitments to central dogmas, as contrasted with
"revealed theology" conceived as dealing with such beliefs as do presuppose such commitments. That is, the one is conceived as moving in the
realm of "reason" and the other in the realm of "faith", in the interest of
one religious tradition. This view is illustrated, of course, in the Thomistic
approach to the Christian faith.

Now the philosophers who have figured in our study are clearly not
committed to the first of these alternative views concerning the relation of
religious philosophy to theology. Each is concerned in his own way to indicate "the" "meaning of God in human experience", to establish a universally valid philosophy of religious faith and practice, a philosophy for
religious *living*. All except Macintosh are professionally designated philosophers rather than theologians and write in terms of "philosophy of
religion." Yet there seems to be an open question as to whether, in their
religious philosophies, they are not actually assuming the validity of certain notions associated with specifically Christian faith and theology. We
have seen that Hocking finds his dialectical interpretation of history as
culminating in an ideal expression of Christianity to be "retrospective",

and that he believes that Christianity in its ideal expression may become the "world-faith". Brightman believes that his idea of a finite God eternally struggling with and overcoming evils in history is essentially the same doctrine as that expressed in the Christian symbols of the Cross, Resurrection, and so on. He further finds the Christian emphasis upon the significance of personality to be uniquely compatible with the major emphases of "personalism" as a philosophy. Are his philosophical views also "retrospective"?

Again, Boodin indicates that he takes his description of "the religion of tomorrow" to be a modern formulation of the religion of Jesus, though we have questioned the compatibility of his dualism with traditional Christian doctrine. Macintosh bases his theology upon an essentially Christian type of religious experience and states that it is "impossible for him to believe" that "Christianity is not essentially true". And Wieman, while disavowing any simple appeal to religious experience of a specific type, suggests that we should seek to determine the appropriate category for deity by rendering explicit the belief "implicit in the living of the most magnificent lives of our Christian tradition". Thus there seems to be considerable indefiniteness on the part of our philosophers concerning the basic question whether their systems claim a universal validity which is reached independently of prior commitments to a particular faith or whether they are actually attempts to offer a philosophical defense of a particular faith which is taken to be universally valid. Do these "natural theologies" presuppose or lead to a "revealed theology", or are they offered as universal natural theologies in terms of which all "revealed" theologies are to be judged? This, we believe, is a question of some importance, and we do not believe that it is clearly answered by those thinkers whose systems we have reviewed.

A new and fruitful way of getting at some of the problems involved in the relation of religious philosophy to theology is suggested, we believe, in the widespread contemporary use of linguistic analysis to reinterpret many of the traditional problems of philosophy. It may well be that, in the expression of religious faith, content is so closely bound to form that an interpretation of the one apart from the other would result in gross distortion. Yet we noted above James' suggestion that an empirical religious philosophy might attempt to dissociate the "literal" from the "symbolic" in its examination and criticism of various beliefs. Some recent remarks of Wieman concerning the relation of philosophy of religion to theology seem to express essentially the same view. We may take them to be illustrative of the general viewpoint implicit in the approach of all the philosophers examined in our study, though the others seem to have written little about the problem as stated in this form.

According to Wieman, it is proper for the theologian to employ linguistic tools used in "preaching, in religious ceremonial, and in private devotion", while the philosopher of religion should "use as the tools for his thinking whatever technical terms seem fitted to designate most accurately the differentia which characterize realities which he is seeking to discriminate and inter-relate". Theological language is properly "emotive", is closely bound up with special historic associations (James' "historic incrustations"?), and is designed to stir up feeling and impel action. It is the task of the theologian to "keep religious words organized and related to all other words in usage so that religious phraseology will make sense and thereby fit for usage by priests and prophets who directly inspire to religious living." The philosopher of religion, on the other hand, should "search out the nature of the religious reality when tradition fails to guide . . . to ascertain with more precision what are the criteria by which one may distinguish the realities which these words in current usage are intended to designate." In other words, his is the definite task of "designating more clearly the kind of happening going on in the world that can be identified with God."[8]

It is interesting to note that Wieman seems to suggest here a semi-apologetic function for religious philosophy, since its operations seem designed to vitalize the concepts of a specific faith "when tradition fails to guide", using as its data religious "words in current usage". But there is the further assumption that by making the "emotive" words "designative" they will be made universally meaningful. This implies that there is no unique truth-value inherent in the "emotive" *forms* as well as in the verbal or behavioral *content* of religious expressions. Other philosophers who have devoted more attention to this problem than have our empirical philosophers have been less certain of the possibility of completely translating religious and theological terms as they function in specific faiths into non-religious philosophical terms which would be at the same time faithful to their religious referents and universally intelligible and valid.

For instance, W. M. Urban has recently presented a most suggestive analysis of the role of "symbolic form" in various areas of philosophical investigation,[9] in which he suggests clear-cut distinctions between scientific, esthetic, and religious symbols. The latter are, like the esthetic, "presentative" or "insight" symbols rather than "representative" or "labelling" as are those of science. The language of religion, he believes, is the language of poetry enhanced by a specific "numinous" quality. It is lyrical and "emotive" or "evocative", indeed, but it is also "invocative", suggesting a referent peculiarly associated with its own form of expression. The language of religion, as Niebuhr has put it, is the language of "poetry which is believed".[10] Furthermore, it is dramatic, employing myths and parables about subjects peculiarly appropriate to religion and inappropriate to science or most forms of philosophy—subjects like the "creation" and "end" of the world and the nature of divine transactions with men.[11] And some religious language, as Richard Kroner has pointed out, cannot be described simply as "dramatic" language. Biblical language, for instance, is the language of a "drama" in which the reader is participant not spectator. Thus it is more nearly yet not quite like the language of epic, involving as it does a fusion of the historical and concrete with the religiously imaginative or "spiritual", in an attempt to create "a picture of life in its universal, therefore permanent, significance."[12]

Because of the peculiar character of religious expression, in which content is inextricably bound up with form and with historical associations, and which seems to imply its own peculiar referent described in terms of "the numinous", Urban believes that "it is probable . . . that the language of religion can never be translated into that of metaphysics without leaving a remainder". The two languages, he believes, constantly tend to merge, yet they live on together in what seems to be perennial "conflict", a conflict which is frequently fruitful for both religion and metaphysics.[13] This conclusion is significant in view of the fact that Urban believes that any area of inquiry is philosophically "explained" only when it is "verbally expanded" or "translated" into metaphysics. Paul Tillich suggests a similar but more radical conclusion differently expressed when he says that the distinguishing characteristic of the religious symbol is its implicit reference to "the unconditioned transcendent", an "ultimate" reality which can be mirrored only in religious symbols, and in them only "brokenly". That is, the religious symbol does not point to something having at the same time an "objective" existence, as Wieman and others imply; it has no "basis" in the empirical-objective order. In his terminology this means that the religious symbol points, not to any specific "being", which would be idolatrous, but rather to "the unconditioned ground of all being".[14]

These interpretations of religious language involve, of course, specific philosophical and religious viewpoints held by the authors mentioned, and other interpretations would vary as these vary. Thus we are not suggesting that any "empirical" approach would necessarily reach the same conclusions. We are suggesting, however, that these and other analyses of religious language reveal special problems associated with any philosophical interpretation of religion which must be made explicit, and that the philosophers who have figured in our study seem not to have given these problems sufficient attention. It is their tendency to minimize the significance and complexity of these issues which is in part responsible for the indefinite relation of their enterprise to theology, "natural" and "revealed". They have devoted chief attention to the interpretation in metaphysical terms of the content of religious experience and belief, with too little attention to the rôle of symbolic form and historical association in the meaning and expression of such belief and practice.

James, whose influence upon our thinkers we have noted at various points, was perhaps at the same time wiser and more "empirical" in this connection. Though we have seen that he, too, would finally distinguish between the "symbolic", "innocent over-belief", and the "literal" in religion, he also points out that

> what religion reports, you must remember, always purports to be a fact of experience; the divine is actually present, it says, and between it and ourselves relations of give and take are actual. If definite perceptions of fact like this cannot stand upon their own feet, surely abstract reasoning cannot give them the support they are in need of. Conceptual processes can class facts, define them, interpret them; but they do not produce them, nor can they reproduce their individuality. . . . Philosophy in this sphere is thus a secondary function, unable to warrant faith's veracity. . . . In all sad sincerity I think we must conclude that the attempt to demonstrate by purely intellectual processes the truth of the deliverance of direct religious experience is absolutely hopeless.[15]

While this statement undoubtedly is colored by intentional exaggeration, it is our belief that the philosophers examined in this study have not fully appreciated and appropriated the "empirical humility" inherent in the philosophic attitude described by James.

NOTES

CHAPTER ONE

1. William James, *A Pluralistic Universe* (New York: Longmans, Green, and Co., 1909), p. 314.
2. John Dewey, "An Empirical Survey of Empiricisms", in *Studies In The History of Ideas*, (New York: Columbia University Press, 1935), Vol. III, pp. 3-22.
3. J. Loewenberg, "What Is Empirical?", *Journal of Philosophy*, XXXVII: 11, May 23, 1940, p. 283.
4. Loewenberg, *op. cit.*, p. 282.
5. For an illuminating discussion of how a difference in emphasis upon "subject-matter" and upon "method" in the interpretation of empiricism affects the conclusions of two philosophers who are on many points in close agreement, see the study of Woodbridge and Dewey by S. P. Lamprecht, *Empiricism and Natural Knowledge*, University of California Publications in Philosophy, Vol. XVI, No. 4, (Berkeley: University of California Press, 1940), pp. 71-94.
6. John M. Moore, *Theories of Religious Experience*, pp. 158-165.
7. Cf. Moore, *op. cit.*; also E. E. Aubrey, "The Authority of Religious Experience Re-examined", *Journal of Religion*, XIII:4, October, 1933, pp. 33-49.
8. P. A. Bertocci, *The Empirical Argument For God In Late British Thought*, (Cambridge: Harvard University Press, 1938), p. 3.
9. J. S. Bixler, *Religion In The Philosophy Of William James*, (Boston: Marshall Jones Company, 1926), 225 pp.

CHAPTER TWO, SECTION I (HOCKING)

1. W. E. Hocking, *The Meaning of God in Human Experience*, (New Haven: Yale University Press, 1912), pp. xix-xx.
2. *Ibid.*, p. 290.
3. Hocking, *Types of Philosophy*, (New York: Charles Scribner's Sons, 1929), p. 449.
4. Hocking, "Some Second Principles", in *Contemporary American Philosophy*, Edited by G. P. Adams and W. P. Montague, (New York: The Macmillan Co., 1930), Vol. I, p. 386. Used by permission.
5. Hocking, *The Meaning of God in Human Experience*, p. 229 .
6. *Ibid.*, p. vi.
7. *Ibid.*, p. xi-xiii.
8. Hocking, *Types of Philosophy*, pp. 175-212.
9. Hocking, *The Meaning Of God In Human Experience*, pp. 172-212.
10. *Ibid.*, pp. 90-99.
11. *Ibid.*, pp. 100-108.
12. *Ibid.*, p. 106.
13. *Ibid.*, p. 236.
14. *Ibid.*, p. 240.
15. *Ibid.*, pp. 287-289; 240-289.
16. *Ibid.*, p. 302.
17. Hocking, *The Meaning Of God In Human Experience*, pp. 356-386.
18. Hocking, *The Meaning of God In Human Experience*, p. 387; Cf. *Types Of Philosophy*, pp. 379-421.

19. "Mysticism As seen through Its Psychology", *Mind*, N.S., XXI: 81, January 1912, pp. 43-44.

20. Moore, *op. cit.*, p. 194. Used by permission.

21. See Moore, *op. cit.*, pp. 190ff.

22. Hocking, *The Meaning Of God In Human Experience*, p. 315; pp. 301-316.

23. *Ibid.*, p. 312.

24. Hocking, *The Meaning Of God In Human Experience*, pp. xiii ff.

25. Cf. Hocking, *Types of Philosophy*, pp. 141-149, 160-164.

26. Hocking, *The Meaning Of God In Human Experience*, p. xv.

27. "Action And Certainty", *Journal of Philosophy*, Vol. XXVII, No. 9, April 24, 1930, pp. 225-238.

28. Hocking, *Types Of Philosophy*, p. 434.

29. *Contemporary American Philosophy*, pp. 394-396.

30. Hocking, *Living Religions and A World Faith*, (New York: The Macmillan Co., 1940), pp. 197-198. Used by permission. Cf. "Dewey's Concepts of Experience and Nature", *Philosophical Review*, XLIX: 2, March, 1940, pp. 235-242.

31. Hocking, *Thoughts On Life And Death*, (New York: Harper and Brothers, 1937), pp. 174-184. See also *What Man Can Make Of Man*, (New York: Harper and Brothers, 1942) *passim*.

32. Hocking, *The Meaning Of God In Human Experience*, p. 477.

33. Hocking, *Thoughts on Life And Death*, p. 95.

34. Hocking, *The Meaning Of God In Human Experience*, pp. 166-206; 220-225; *Types Of Philosophy*, pp. 372ff.; *Contemporary American Philosophy*, pp. 398-400.

35. Hocking, *The Meaning Of God In Human Experience*, pp. 330-332.

36. Hocking, *The Meaning Of God In Human Experience*, pp. 225-226.

37. *Ibid.*, p. 226; 335-337.

38. Hocking, *Thoughts On Life And Death*, pp. 186-192; 145-232.

39. "The Illicit Naturalising of Religion", *Journal of Religion*, III:6, November, 1923, pp. 561-589.

40. Hocking, *Living Religions and A World Faith*, (New York: The Macmillan Co., 1940), pp. 215-224. Used by permission.

41. Cf. *Morale And Its Enemies, 1918, Present Status of the Philosophy of Law and of Rights*, 1926, and *Man And The State*, 1926, (New Haven: Yale University Press).

42. Hocking, *The Self, Its Body and Freedom*, (New Haven: Yale University Press, 1928), pp. 3-97; 146-161; *Thoughts On Life and Death*, pp. 51-85.

43. Hocking, *The Lasting Elements of Individualism*, (New Haven: Yale University Press, 1937), *passim*.

44. Hocking, *What Man Can Make Of Man*, pp. 4-7.

45. Hocking, *Human Nature and Its Remaking*, (New Haven: Yale University Press, 1918), pp. 29-33.

46. Cf. Royce, *The Problem of Christianity*.

47. Hocking, *Human Nature and Its Remaking*, cc. XXV-XL.

48. *Ibid.*, p. 398.

49. *Ibid.*, pp. 392-401.

50. *Ibid.*, p. 403.

51. Hocking, *Living Religions and a World Faith*, p. 191.

52. Hocking, *Living Religions and a World Faith*, pp. 23-63; 143-265.

CHAPTER TWO, SECTION TWO (BRIGHTMAN)

1. Article by Edgar Sheffield Brightman in *Contemporary American Theology*, I, ed. by Vergilius Ferm, used by permission.

2. E. S. Brightman, *A Philosophy of Religion*, (New York: Prentice-Hall, Inc., 1940), p. 8.

3. Brightman, *A Philosophy of Religion*, p. 1.

4. Brightman, *Moral Laws*, (New York: The Abingdon Press, 1933), pp. 56-57.

5. Brightman, *A Philosophy of Religion*, p. 529.

6. *Ibid.*, p. 163.

7. *Ibid.*, p. 347.

8. *Ibid.*, pp. 165-167.

9. *Ibid.*, pp. 348-349.

10. *Ibid.*, cf. "What is Personality?", *The Personalist*, XX:2, April, 1939, pp. 129-138.

11. Brightman, *A Philosophy of Religion*, p. 350.

12. *Ibid.*, pp. 350-351.

13. Brightman, *Personality and Religion*, (New York: The Abingdon Press, 1934), pp. 16-19.

14. Brightman, *A Philosophy of Religion*, p. 349.

15. Brightman, *An Introduction to Philosophy*, (New York: Henry Holt and Co., 1925), pp. 49-50; pp. 89ff. Cf. "The More-Than-Human Values of Religion", *Journal of Religion*, I:4, July, 1921, pp. 376-377; *Personality and Religion*, pp. 26-29. We may suggest that Brightman himself apparently avoids solipsism only by appealing to inference, "the demands of action and reason". The concept of externality is thus precariously maintained. It is difficult to see how, if one limits knowledge in Lockian fashion to "agreement and disagreement of ideas", he can avoid the various stages leading from this position to solipsism as outlined by Professor W. P. Montague in his *The Ways of Knowing*, (New York: The Macmillan Co., 1936), Chs. IX-X.

16. Brightman, *A Philosophy of Religion*, p. 353; Ferm (Ed.), *Contemporary American Theology*, pp. 58-60; Brightman, *An Introduction to Philosophy*, pp. 60ff.

17. Brightman, *The Spiritual Life*, (New York: Abingdon-Cokesbury Press, 1942) p. 33.

18. Ferm, (Ed.), *Contemporary American Theology*, pp. 61-63.

19. Brightman, *A Philosophy of Religion*, p. 415.

20. Brightman, *Religious Values*, (New York: The Abingdon Press, 1925), pp. 190ff; *The Spiritual Life*, pp. 126-131.

21. Brightman, *Religious Values*, p. 9.

22. Brightman, *A Philosophy of Religion*, pp. 436-437.

23. Brightman, *The Problem of God*, (New York: The Abingdon Press, 1930), pp. 160-161; cf. *The Finding of God*, (New York: The Abingdon Press, 1931), pp. 94-114.

24. "The Dialectic of Religious Experience", *Philosophical Review*, XXXVIII: 6, November, 1929, pp. 557-573.

25. Brightman, *A Philosophy of Religion*, p. 193.

26. Brightman, *Introduction to Philosophy*, pp. 12-29.

27. "What Constitutes a Scientific Philosophy of Religion?", *Journal of Religion*, VI: 3, May 1926, pp. 250-258.

28. Brightman, *Is God a Person?*, (New York: Association Press, 1932), pp. 27-29.

29. "An Empirical Approach to God", *The Philosophical Review*, XLVI: 2, March, 1937, pp. 147-151.

30. Ferm, (Ed.), *Contemporary American Theology*, pp. 67-69.

31. *Ibid.*, pp. 69-71.

32. Brightman, *The Finding of God*, pp. 17-23.

33. Brightman, *A Philosophy of Religion*, p. 1.

34. *Ibid.*, pp. 6-7.

35. Brightman, *Personality and Religion*, pp. 86-90.

36. "An Empirical Approach to God", *op. cit.*, pp. 154-155.

37. "From Rationalism to Empiricism", in the series "How My Mind Has Changed in This Decade", *The Christian Century*, LVI: 9, March 1, 1939, p. 276.

38. *Ibid.*, pp. 276-77.

39. Brightman, *Personality and Religion*, p. 92.

40. Loewenberg, *op. cit.*, passim.

41. Brightman, *Introduction to Philosophy*, p. 246.

42. "The Definition of Idealism", *Journal of Philosophy*, XXX: 16, August 3, 1933, p. 434.

43. "Personalism and the Influence of Bowne", in *Proceedings of the Sixth International*

Congress of Philosophy, Ed. E. S. Brightman, (New York: Longmans, Green, and Co., 1927), pp. 161-162.

44. Brightman, A Philosophy of Religion, p. 3.
45. Ibid., pp. 182ff.
46. Brightman, Religious Values, p. 58.
47. Brightman, Moral Laws, pp. 53-54.
48. Ibid., pp. 86-90.
49. Brightman, Religious Values, p. 15; cf. A Philosophy of Religion, p. 88; The Spiritual Life, p. 65.
50. Brightman, Religious Values, p. 15; cf. A Philosophy of Religion, p. 93.
51. Brightman, A Philosophy of Ideals, (New York: Henry Holt and Co., 1928), pp. 68-75.
52. Ibid., pp. 88-97.
53. Brightman, The Spiritual Life, pp. 119-120.
54. Ibid., p. 116.
55. Ibid., p. 118.
56. Ibid., p. 123.
57. Brightman, A Philosophy of Ideals, pp. 75ff.
58. Brightman, A Philosophy of Religion, pp. 99-100.
59. Ibid., p. 104.
60. Brightman, Religious Values, pp. 107-136.
61. Brightman, A Philosophy of Religion, pp. 251-259.
62. Brightman's interest in the Ritschlian approach is reflected in his earliest writings, specifically in his doctoral dissertation on "Ritschl's Criterion of Truth"—published in typescript, Boston, 1921; summarized in Art., American Journal of Theology, XXI; 2, April, 1917, pp. 212-224.
63. Brightman, The Problem of God, pp. 150-156; The Finding of God, pp. 101-107; Introduction to Philosophy., pp. 281-314.
64. Brightman, The Problem of God, pp. 116-120; A Philosophy of Religion. pp. 226-232; The Spiritual Life, pp. 131-134.
65. Brightman, A Philosophy of Religion, pp. 363-369.
66. Brightman, The Problem of God, pp. 120-122.
67. Brightman, A Philosophy of Religion, pp. 204-207.
68. Ibid., pp. 319-321.
69. "An Empirical Approach to God", op. cit., pp. 153ff.
70. Ibid., p. 545.
71. Brightman, The Finding of God, pp. 125-134.
72. Brightman, The Problem of God, pp. 131-137.
73. Brightman, The Finding of God, pp. 120-122. Brightman states that he was actually led to the concept of the finite God primarily by careful attention to the facts of evolution, and subsequently found that religious experience confirms the idea.—The Problem of God, p. 176.
74. Brightman, A Philosophy of Religion, pp. 305-321.
75. Brightman, The Problem of God, p. 113.
76. Brightman, Is God a Person?, p. 81.
77. "An Empirical Approach to God", op. cit.
78. Brightman, A Philosophy of Religion, p. 213.
79. For a summary of the major types, see Art., Religion in Life, I:1, pp. 134ff.
80. De Burgh, W.G., review of A Philosophy of Religion, Mind, N.S., XLIX: 196, October, 1940, pp. 483ff.
81. Ibid., p. 486.
82. Brightman, A Philosophy of Religion, pp. 324-335.
83. Cf. S. P. Lamprecht, review of P. A. Bertocci's The Empirical Argument for God in Late British Thought, in the Journal of Philosophy, XXXVI: 3, Feb. 2, 1939; also discussion in XXXVI: 10, May 11, 1939, pp. 263-274.

CHAPTER TWO, SECTION THREE (BOODIN)

1. Boodin, J.E., *Truth and Reality*, (New York: The Macmillan Co., 1911).
2. Boodin, J.E., *A Realistic Universe*, (New York: The Macmillan Co., 1916, Revised Edition 1931). Used by permission.
3. Boodin, *Cosmic Evolution*, (New York: The Macmillan Co., 1925).
4. Boodin, *God and Creation*, (New York: The Macmillan Co., 1934); Two Vols., Vol. I, *Three Interpretations of the Universe*, Vol. II, *God*. Used by permission. Also *Religion of Tomorrow*, (New York: The Philosophical Library, 1943) General Reference for the paragraph—*Contemporary American Philosophy*, *op. cit.*, Vol. I, pp. 136-142; cf. *Three Interpretations of the Universe*, pp. 6-7.
5. Boodin, *Truth and Reality*, p. 280.
6. Boodin, "Functional Realism", in *The Philosophical Review*, XLIII: 2, March, 1934, pp. 147-178.
7. Boodin, *A Realistic Universe*, p. vii.
8. Boodin, *Truth and Reality*, pp. 251-268.
9. Boodin, *Religion of Tomorrow*, p. 26.
10. *Ibid.*, p. 87.
11. *Ibid.*, p. 32.
12. Boodin, *God*, pp. 25-27.
13. *Ibid.*, pp. 27-32.
14. Boodin, *Religion of Tomorrow*, pp. 55, 56.
15. Boodin, *Truth and Reality*, pp. 307ff.
16. Boodin, *Religion of Tomorrow*, p. 46.
17. *Ibid.*, pp. 105-106.
18. Boodin, *Truth and Reality*, p. 326.
19. Boodin, *Religion of Tomorrow*, Preface; cf. pp. 115-153.
20. Boodin, *Truth and Reality*, pp. 251-260; 297-306; *God*, pp. 130-139.
21. Boodin, *God*, pp. 32-43.
22. Boodin, *God*, pp. 99-129.
23. Boodin, *Three Interpretations of the Universe*, p. 88; pp. 15-88.
24. *Ibid.*, pp. 428-84.
25. *Ibid.*, pp. 426-27; 227-324; 420-428.
26. Boodin, *God*, pp. 164-204.
27. *Ibid.*, pp. 145-146.
28. Boodin, *God* pp. 45-50.
29. *Ibid.*, pp. 54ff.
30. Schneider, H.W., "Theology and Science in Contemporary Platonic Idealism", *Review of Religion*, II:2, January, 1938, pp. 166-174.

CHAPTER THREE, SECTION ONE (MACINTOSH)

1. Macintosh, *Theology as an Empirical Science*, (New York: The Macmillan Co., 1919; reprinted 1927). Used by permission.
2. Article by Douglas Clyde Macintosh in *Contemporary American Theology*, I, ed. by Vergilius Ferm, used by permission.
3. Macintosh, *Personal Religion*, (New York: Charles Scribner's Sons, 1942), Part I, pp. 1-174.
4. *Ibid.*, p. 243.
5. *Ibid.*, p. 315.
6. *Ibid.*, p. 323.
7. *Contemporary American Theology*, pp. 277-323.
8. Macintosh, "Personal Idealism, Pragmatism, and the New Realism," *American Journal of Theology*, XIV: October, 1910, p. 656.

9. Macintosh, *The Problem of Religious Knowledge*, (New York: Harper and Bros., 1940), p. 3. Cf. *Theology as an Empirical Science*, p. 239.

10. Macintosh, *The Problem of Knowledge*, (New York: The Macmillan Co., 1915), p. 7.

11. *Ibid.*, pp. 75-96.

12. "The Religious Philosophy of W.E. Hocking", *Yale Divinity Quarterly*, X:3, January, 1914, pp. 73-78; "Hocking's Philosophy of Religion", *Philosophical Review*, XXIII: January, 1914, pp. 27-47; *The Problem of Knowledge*, pp. 164-173.

13. Macintosh, *The Pilgrimage of Faith in the World of Modern Thought*, (Calcutta: University of Calcutta, 1931), pp. 143-153; 263-264; "The Next Step in the Epistemological Dialectic", *Journal of Philosophy*, XXVI: April 1929, pp. 226-227.

14. Macintosh, *The Problem of Knowledge*, pp. 116-118, 225-227; *The Problem of Religious Knowledge*, pp. 84-94.

15. Macintosh, *The Problem of Knowledge*, pp. 219-220.

16. *Ibid.*, p. 56; Cf. *The Reasonableness of Christianity*, (New York: Charles Scribners' Sons, 1925), pp. 196-198.

17. Macintosh, *The Problem of Knowledge*, p. 311; *The Pilgrimage of Faith*, pp. 210ff.

18. *Ibid.*, Cf. *The Problem of Religious Knowledge*, p. 1; For an able dualistic criticism of this view see P. A. Bertocci, "Macintosh's Theory of Natural Knowledge", pp. 164-172.

19. Macintosh, *The Problem of Knowledge*, pp. 312-314, 322-328.

20. *Ibid.*, pp. 344-349; *Religious Realism* (Ed. D.C. Macintosh), (New York: The Macmillan Co., 1931), pp. 361ff.

21. Macintosh, "Empirical Theology and Some of its Misunderstanders", *Review of Religion*, III: 4, May, 1939, pp. 395ff.

22. Macintosh, *The Problem of Knowledge*, p. 350.

23. Macintosh, *The Problem of Religious Knowledge*, p. 175.

24. Macintosh, *The Problem of Knowledge*, p. 409.

25. In this connection Macintosh asks whether the proposition stating such a thesis is itself subject to its own implications. *Ibid.*, pp. 422-430.

26. Macintosh, *The Problem of Knowledge,* pp. 438-447; *The Reasonableness of Christianity*, pp. 210ff.

27. Macintosh, *The Problem of Knowledge*, pp. 432-458; *The Problem of Religious Knowledge*, pp. 6, 306.

28. Macintosh, *The Problem of Knowledge*, pp. 472-494.

29. Eugene G. Bewkes, "Common Sense Realism", in *The Nature of Religious Experience*, (Ed. J.S. Bixler, R.L. Calhoun, and H.R. Niebuhr), (New York: Harper and Bros., 1937), pp. 1-25; cf. "Empirical Theology and Some of its Misunderstanders", *Review of Religion*, III: 4, May 1939, p. 386.

30. Macintosh, *The Reasonableness of Christianity*, p. 163.

31. Macintosh, Cf. *The Problem of Religious Knowledge*, pp. 9-10.

32. *Ibid.*, pp. 15-38, 178-180; "Hocking's Philosophy of Religion", in *The Philosophical Review, op. cit.*, pp. 36-41.

33. Macintosh, *The Problem of Religious Knowledge*, pp. 241-242; cf. *Theology as an Empirical Science*, pp. 14-17.

34. Macintosh, *The Problem of Religious Knowledge*, pp. 243-251; *Theology as an Empirical Science*, pp. 18ff.; see also "Theology in a Scientific Age", in *Education for Christian Service* (Faculty of the Divinity School of Yale University), (New Haven: Yale University Press, 1922), pp. 147-149. Also, for a general estimate of Schleiermacher and Ritschl as well as of the general role of religious experience in the history of Christian theology, see Macintosh's doctoral (Chicago: University of Chicago, 1911 86pp.) dissertation, *The Reaction Against Metaphysics in Theology*.

35. Macintosh, *The Problem of Religious Knowledge*, p. 163; cf. *Theology as an Empirical Science*, p. 245.

36. Macintosh, "Religious Values and the Existence of God", *Journal of Religion*, VI: May 1926, pp. 315-318; *The Problem of Religious Knowledge*, p. 8.

37. *Ibid.*, p. 164; cf. *Religious Realism*, (New York; The Macmillan Co., 1931), pp. 308ff.

38. Macintosh, "Theology, Valuational or Existential?", *Review of Religion*, IV: 1, November, 1939, pp. 41-44.
39. Macintosh, *Religious Realism*, pp. 337-338.
40. Macintosh, *The Problem of Religious Knowledge*, p. 165.
41. Cf. P.A. Bertocci, "An Analysis of Macintosh's Theory of Religious Knowledge", *The Journal of Religion*, XXIV: 1, January, 1944, pp. 42-55.
42. Macintosh, *The Problem of Religious Knowledge*, p. 178.
43. *Ibid.*, pp. 171ff.; cf. *The Reasonableness of Christianity*, pp. 236ff., *The Pilgrimmage of Faith*, pp. 217ff., *Theology as an Empirical Science*, pp. 144ff.
44. Macintosh, *Theology as an Empirical Science*, p. 142.
45. Macintosh, *Personal Religion*, p. 159.
46. *Ibid.*, pp. 160-161.
47. Macintosh, *The Reasonableness of Christianity*, p. 324.
48. C.C. Morrison, Editor, *Is There a God?* (Chicago: Willett, Clark, and Co., 1932), pp. 289-294.
49. Macintosh, *Personal Religion*, p. 161.
50. Macintosh, *Theology as an Empirical Science*, p. 142.
51. Macintosh, *Personal Religion*, p. 216.
52. *Ibid.*, p. 217.
53. *Ibid.*, pp. 217-219.
54. Macintosh, *The Problem of Religious Knowledge*, p. 191; cf. *Theology as an Empirical Science*, p. 246.
55. Macintosh, *Theology as an Empirical Science*, pp. 27-41.
56. Macintosh, *Personal Religion*, p. 215; cf. "Professor Coe and an Empirical Theology", *The Methodist Quarterly Review*, LXXVI: April, 1927, pp. 211-213; "Is Belief in the Historicity of Jesus Indispensable to the Christian Faith?", *Americal Journal of Theology*, XV: July, 1911, pp. 362-372.
57. Macintosh, *Theology as an Empirical Science*, pp. 68-92; cf. "Professor Coe and an Empirical Theology", *op. cit.*, pp. 202-210.
58. Macintosh, *Theology as an Empirical Science*, pp. 31-34.
59. *Ibid.*, p. 109.
60. Cf. Macintosh, *The Problem of Religious Knowledge*, pp. 202-209, *Theology as an Empirical Science*, pp. 140-156.
61. "Religious Knowledge and Religious Faith", *Colgate-Rochester Divinity School Bulletin*, II: November, 1929, pp. 160-174; cf. *Theology as an Empirical Science*, pp. 159ff., *The Problem of Religious Knowledge*, pp. 212ff.
62. See the essays of J.S. Bixler and H.R. Niebuhr, in *The Nature of Religious Experience*, *op. cit.* cf. Macintosh's reply, "Theology, Valuation or Existential?" *Review of Religion*, IV: 1, November, 1939, pp. 22-41.
63. Macintosh, *The Reasonableness of Christianity*, p. 242.
64. *Ibid.*, pp. 46ff.
65. *Ibid.*, pp. 19-24; cf. *The Problem of Religious Knowledge*, p. 362.
66. *Education for Christian Service*, *op. cit.*, pp. 151-152.
67. *Contemporary American Theology*, op. cit., p. 312.
68. Macintosh, *The Problem of Religious Knowledge*, pp. 225-229; *Is There a God?*, p. 212.
69. Macintosh, *The Reasonableness of Christianity*, p. 128.
70. Cf. "Mr. Wieman and Mr. Macintosh Converse with Mr. Dewey", *The Christian Century*, L: March, 1, 1933, p. 301.
71. Macintosh, *Theology as an Empirical Science*, pp. 92-97.
72. Macintosh, *God in a World at War*, (London: George Allen and Unwin, Ltd., 1918), pp. 38-40; cf. *The Reasonableness of Christianity*, pp. 90-104; *Theology as an Empirical Science*, pp. 216ff.
73. Macintosh, "What Has Professor Brightman Done to Personalism?", *Religion in Life*, I: Spring, 1932, pp. 304-307.
74. Macintosh, *The Reasonableness of Christianity*, pp. 78-79; *Religious Realism*, pp.

395-404; *The Problem of Religious Knowledge*, pp. 170, 358-360; cf. also "What God Is", in *My Idea of God*, edited by J.F. Newton, (Boston: Little, Brown, and Co., 1927), pp. 137-158.

75. Macintosh, "The New Christianity and World Conversion", *American Journal of Theology*, XVIII: October, 1914, pp. 555-557; *Theology as an Empirical Science*, pp. 256-257.

76. Macintosh, *Theology as an Empirical Science*, pp. 258ff.; *The Reasonableness of Christianity*, pp. 276ff.; *The Problem of Religious Knowledge*, pp. 377ff.

77. "The Spirit and the Life", *Review of Religion*, I: 2, January, 1937, p. 120.

78. Cf. *The Pilgrimmage of Faith*, pp. 8-18, 225-229.

79. Macintosh, *The Problem of Religious Knowledge*, pp. 196-199.

80. "Empirical Theology and Some of its Misunderstanders", *Review of Religion*, III: 4, May, 1939, pp. 395-397. Cf. *Personal Religion*, pp. 207-229.

CHAPTER THREE, SECTION TWO (WIEMAN)

1. Article by Henry Nelson Wieman, in *Contemporary American Theology*, I, ed. by Virgilius Ferm, used by permission.

2. Wieman, *Religious Experience and Scientific Method*, (New York: The Macmillan Co., 1926; 2nd. Ed. 1927), p. 6.

3. *Contemporary American Theology, op. cit.*, pp. 345-346.

4. "Some Blind Spots Removed", in the series "How My Mind Has Changed in This Decade", *The Christian Century*, LVI: 4, Jan. 25, 1939, pp. 116-118.

5. Points of agreement between Macintosh and Wieman have been summarised by Macintosh in *The Problem of Religious Knowledge, op. cit.*, pp. 165ff.

6. With M.C. Otto and D.C. Macintosh, *Is There a God?*, (Chicago: Willett, Clark, and Co., 1932), p. 276.

7. Wieman, *Religious Experience and Scientific Method*, p. 9. Used by permission.

8. "God, the Inescapable", *The Christian Century*, XLVIII: 38, 39, Sept. 23 and 30, 1931, pp. 1170-1172, 1209-1221.

9. With W. M. Horton, *The Growth of Religion*, (Chicago: Willett, Clark, and Co., 1938), pp. 258-259.

10. "God is More Than We Can Think", *Christendom*, I: 3, Spring, 1936, p. 438.

11. Review of *The Nature of Religious Experience, op. cit.*, in *Christendom*, II:3, Summer, 1937, pp. 497-501.

12. Wieman, *Growth of Religion*, pp. 423-426.

13. Review of Brightman's *A Philosophy of Religion*, in *The Journal of Religion*, XXI: 2, April, 1941, pp. 198-200.

14. "Religion in John Dewey's Philosophy", *The Journal of Religion*, XI: I, January 1931, pp. 3-4.

15. "The Power and Goodness of God", *The Journal of Religion*, XXIII: 4, October, 1943, pp. 266-267.

16. *The Journal of Religion*, XXIV: 1, January, 1944, p. 57.

17. "Experience, Mind, and the Concept", *Journal of Philosophy*, XXI: 21, Oct. 9, 1924, pp. 561-567.

18. "How Do We Know God", *The Journal of Religion*, V: 2, March, 1925, pp. 113-117.

19. Wieman, *The Wrestle of Religion with Truth*, (New York: The Macmillan Co., 1927), pp. 24ff., *The Growth of Religion, op. cit.*, pp. 386-390.

20. "Perception and Cognition", *The Journal of Philosophy*, XL: 3, Feb. 4, 1943, pp. 74-75.

21. *Ibid.*, p. 74.

22. "Can God Be Perceived?", *The Journal of Religion*, XXIII: 1, January, 1943, pp. 26-29.

23. Wieman, *Religious Experience and Scientific Method*, p. 29; cf. "How Do We Know God?", *The Journal of Religion*, V: 2, March, 1925, pp. 115-118.

24. H. H. Dubs, "Religious Naturalism—An Evaluation", *The Journal of Religion*, XXIII: 4, October, 1943), p. 258.

25. Wieman, *Religious Experience and Scientific Method*, pp. 35-40. Used by permission.

26. Wieman, *Religious Experience and Scientific Method*, pp. 341-352; used by permission. Cf. "Religion in Dewey's Experience and Nature", *The Journal of Religion*, V: 5, September, 1925, pp. 519-542.

27. Wieman, *Methods of Private Religious Living*, (New York: The Macmillan Co., 1938); earlier editions 1929, 1931; pp. 183-195, 22-30; cf. (With R.P. Wieman) *Normative Psychology of Religion*, (New York: Thomas Y. Crowell Co., 1935), pp. 173-192; Wieman, *The Issues of Life*, (New York: The Abingdon Press, 1930), pp. 18-28.

28. Wieman, *Normative Psychology of Religion*, pp. 185ff.

29. Wieman, *The Wrestle of Religion with Truth*, pp. 153ff.

30. Wieman, *The Wrestle of Religion with Truth*, pp. 153-156.

31. *Christendom*, II: 2, Spring, 1937, pp. 213ff.

32. Cf. W.H. Bernhardt, "The Cognitive Quest for God", *The Journal of Religion*, XXIII: 2, April, 1943, pp. 91ff.

33. "Values: Primary Data for Religious Inquiry", *Journal of Religion*, XVI: 4, October, 1936, pp. 379-380.

34. Review of H.P. Van Dusen's *The Plain Man Seeks for God*, *Journal of Religion*, XIV: 1, January, 1934, pp. 117-118.

35. Wieman, *Normative Psychology of Religion*, p. 46.

36. "Values: Primary Data for Religious Inquiry", *op. cit.*, pp. 380-399; cf. "Value and the Individual", *Journal of Philosophy*, XXV: 9, April 26, 1928, pp. 233-239.

37. "Religion in John Dewey's Philosophy", *Journal of Religion*, XL:1, January 1931, p. 12, pp. 11-18.

38. Wieman, *Religious Experience and Scientific Method*, pp. 272-278; cf. reviews of R.T. Flewelling, *Creative Personality*, and Albert C. Knudson *The Philosophy of Personalism*, *Journal of Religion*, VII: 7, pp. 321ff., VIII:2, pp. 291ff.

39. Dewey, "The Satisfying and the Valuable", in *The Quest for Certainty*, pp. 260-281; reprinted in Joseph Ratner, ed., *Intelligence in the Modern World: John Dewey's Philosophy*, (New York: The Modern Library, 1939), p. 785.

40. Wieman, *The Growth of Religion*, p. 270; cf. *Methods of Private Religious Living*, pp. 207-212.

41. Wieman, *Religious Experience and Scientific Method*, pp. 32-33. Used by permission.

42. *Ibid.*, p. 23.

43. *Ibid.*, pp. 160-176.

44. "Authority and the Normative Approach", *Journal of Religion*, XVI: 2, April, 1936, p. 184.

45. Pamphlet, "The Scientific Method and the Christian Gospel", (Madison, New Jersey: Conference of Theological Schools, 1929), pp. 4-5.

46. "Another Interpretation of Saint Francis," *The Christian Century*, XLVII: 7, Feb. 12, 1930, pp. 206-211.

47. Wieman, *The Issues of Life*, pp. 184ff.

48. Wieman, *The Wrestle of Religion with Truth*, pp. 63ff.; *Methods of Private Religious Living*, pp. 196ff.

49. Wieman, *Religious Experience and Scientific Method*, p. 46.

50. "The Scientific Method and the Christian Gospel", *op. cit.*, p. 6.

51. Wieman, *The Wrestle of Religion with Truth*, pp. 63-67.

52. Wieman, *The Issues of Life*, pp. 184-188.

53. "Authority and the Normative Approach", *op. cit.*, pp. 185ff.

54. "Right Ways to Justify Religion", *The Christian Century*, XLVII: 5, Jan. 29, 1930, pp. 139-142.

55. "God is More Than We Can Think", *op. cit.*, pp. 435-437.

56. Cf. "How Do We Know?", *The Christian Century*, XLVIII: 21, May 27, 1931, pp. 711-715.

57. Wieman, *Is There a God?*, p. 13; Cf. J. H. Randall, Jr., "The Religion of Shared Experience", in *The Philosopher of the Common Man: Essays in Honor of John Dewey;* (New York: G. P. Putnam's Sons, 1940), pp. 106-146.
58. *Contemporary American Theology*, op. cit., p. 351.
59. Wieman, *The Wrestle of Religion with Truth, op. cit.*, pp. 179-212.
60. Wieman, *The Wrestle of Religion with Truth*, p. 161.
61. Wieman, *The Growth of Religion*, pp. 266-267.
62. Wieman, *The Growth of Religion*, pp. 325-367; cf. *Normative Psychology of Religion*, pp. 50-55; "Values: Primary Data for Religious Inquiry", *op. cit.*, pp. 403-405.
63. "The Power and Goodness of God", *The Journal of Religion*, XXIII: 4, October, 1943, pp. 269-272.
64. *The Christian Century*, LI: 49, Dec. 5, 1941, pp. 1551-1552.
65. R. L. Calhoun, "The Power of God and the Wisdom of God", *Christendom*, II: 1, Winter, 1937, pp. 37ff.; cf. "A Final Statement", *op. cit.*, II: 2, Spring, 1937, pp. 215-217.
66. "Faith and Knowledge", *Christendom*, I: 5, Autumn, 1936, p. 765.
67. For other statements of some of these objections directed against a view similar to that of Wieman as held by E. R. Walker, see the articles of George Thomas, John C. Bennett, and David E. Roberts in *The Journal of Religion*, XX:2, April, 1940, pp. 169-177.
68. Wieman, *The Issues of Life*, pp. 219-230; *Is There a God?*, pp. 48ff.; *Contemporary American Theology, op. cit.*, pp. 349-351; *The Growth of Religion*, pp. 359-362.
69. "God is More Than We Can Think" and "Faith and Knowledge", *Christendom*, I: 3, 5; Spring and Autumn, 1936, pp. 432, 777-778.
70. Wieman, *The Growth of Religion*, pp. 268; 357-359; *The Wrestle of Religion with Truth*, pp. 200-203; *Methods of Private Religious Living*, p. 58.

CHAPTER FOUR

1. Moore, op. cit., pp. 225-226.
2. Cf. John Dewey, *Experience and Nature* (Chicago: Open Court Publishing Co., 1925), Chapter 1; *Logic: The Theory of Inquiry*, (New York: Henry Holt and Co., 1938), Chapter XXI.
3. John Dewey, *A Common Faith*, (New Haven: Yale University Press, 1934).
4. William James, *The Varieties of Religious Experience* (New York: The Modern Library, N.D.) p. 445.
5. Cf. H.W. Schneider, "Radical Empiricism In Religion", in *Essays in Honor of John Dewey*, (New York: Henry Holt and Co., 1929.) pp. 377ff.
6. James, *op. cit.*, p. 446.
7. James, *op. cit.*, p. 446.
8. "Theology and the Philosophy of Religion", *Journal of Liberal Religion*, II: 4, Spring, 1941, pp. 167-172.
9. W.M. Urban, *Language and Reality*, (London: George Allen and Unwin, Ltd., 1939) 755pp.
10. Cf. Rheinhold Niebuhr, "The Truth of Myths", in *The Nature of Religious Experience, op. cit.*, p. 117ff.
11. Urban, *op. cit.*, pp. 580ff.
12. Richard Kroner, *How Do We Know God?* (New York: Harper and Bros., 1943) pp. 118ff.
13. Urban, *op. cit.*, pp. 626-628.
14. (Paul Tillich, "The Religious Symbol", *Journal of Liberal Religion*, II:1, Summer, 1940), pp. 13ff.
15. James, *op. cit.*, p. 445.

BIBLIOGRAPHY

SPECIAL AUTHORS

BOODIN, JOHN ELOF

Books

A Realistic Universe. New York: The Macmillan Co., 1916. 412pp.
Cosmic Evolution. New York: The Macmillan Co., 1925. 484pp.
God and Creation. New York: The Macmillan Co., 1934. Two Vols.: Vol. I, *Three Interpretations of the Universe:* Vol. II, *God.*
Religion of Tomorrow. New York: The Philosophical Library, 1943. 189pp.
The Social Mind. New York: The Macmillan Co., 1939. 593pp.
Truth and Reality. New York: The Macmillan Co., 1911. 334pp.

Essays

"God and Cosmic Structure", *The Development of American Philosophy*, Walter E. Muelder and Laurence Sears, Editors; New York: Houghton Mifflin Co., 1940.
"God and the Cosmos", *Religious Realism*, D. C. Macintosh, Editor; New York: The Macmillan Co., 1931. Pp. 479-495.
"Nature and Reason", *Contemporary American Philosophy*, G. P. Adams and W. P. Montague, Editors; New York: The Macmillan Co., 1930. Two Vols., Vol. I, Pp. 136-166.

Periodical Article

"Functional Realism", *The Philosophical Review*, XLIII:2, March, 1934. Pp. 147-178.

BRIGHTMAN, EDGAR SHEFFIELD

Books

A Philosophy of Ideals. New York: Henry Holt and Co., 1928. 218pp.
A Philosophy of Religion. New York: Prentice-Hall Inc., 1940. 489pp.
An Introduction to Philosophy. New York: Henry Holt and Co., 1925. 364pp.
Is God a Person?. New York: Association Press, 1932. 87pp.
Moral Laws. New York: The Abingdon Press, 1933. 322pp.
Personality and Religion. New York: The Abingdon Press, 1934. 156pp.
Religious Values. New York: The Abingdon Press, 1925. 277pp.
The Finding of God. New York: The Abingdon Press, 1931. 193pp.
The Future of Christianity. New York: The Abingdon Press, 1937. 154pp.

The Problem of God. New York: The Abingdon Press, 1930. 193pp.
The Spiritual Life. New York: Abingdon-Cokesbury Press, 1942. 213pp.

Essays

"Personalism and the Influence of Bowne", *Proceedings of the Sixth International Congress of Philosophy.* E. S. Brightman, Editor; New York: Longmans, Green, and Co., 1927. Pp. 161-162.

"Religion As Truth", *Contemporary American Theology.* Vergilius Ferm, editor; New York: Round Table Press, 1932. Two Vols., Vol. I, Pp. 53-85.

"The Dialectical Unity of Consciousness and the Metaphysics of Religion", *Proceedings of the Seventh International Congress of Philosophy.* G. Ryle, editor: London: Humphrey Milford, Oxford University Press, 1931. Pp. 70-77.

Periodical Articles

"A Temporalist View of God", *The Journal of Religion*, XII:4, October, 1932. Pp. 545-555.

"An Empirical Approach to God", *The Philosophical Review*, XLVI:2, March, 1937. Pp. 147-169.

"From Rationalism to Empiricism", *The Christian Century*, LVI:9, March 1, 1939. Pp. 276-279.

"Professor Macintosh on Personalism", *Religion in Life*, I: 1932. Pp. 461-463.

Review of Douglas C. Macintosh, *The Problem of Religious Knowledge, The Journal of Bible and Religion*, IX:1, February, 1941. Pp. 53-56.

Review of Henry N. Wieman and Walter M. Horton, *The Growth of Religion, The Christian Advocate*, CXIV:2, Jan. 12, 1939. P. 30.

"Ritschl's Criterion of Religious Truth", *American Journal of Theology*, XXI:2, April, 1917. Pp. 212-224.

"The Definition of Idealism", *The Journal of Philosophy*, XXX:16, August 3, 1933. Pp. 429-435.

"The Dialectic of Religious Experience", *The Philosophical Review*, XXXVIII:6, November, 1929. Pp. 557-573.

"The Given and its Critics", *Religion in Life*, I:1, January, 1932. Pp. 134-145.

"The More-Than-Human Values of Religion", *The Journal of Religion*, I:4, July, 1921. Pp. 362-377.

"What Constitutes a Scientific Philosophy of Religion?", *The Journal of Religion*, VI:3, May, 1926. Pp. 250-258.

"What is Personality?", *The Personalist*, XX:2, April, 1939. Pp. 129-138.

HOCKING, WILLIAM ERNEST

Books

Human Nature and its Remaking. New Haven: Yale University Press, 1918. 434pp.

Living Religions and a World Faith. New York: The Macmillan Co., 1940. 269pp.

Man and the State. New Haven: Yale University Press, 1926. 455pp.

Morale and its Enemies. New Haven: Yale University Press, 1918. 200pp.

The Lasting Elements of Individualism. New Haven: Yale University Press, 1937. 181pp.

The Meaning of God in Human Experience. New Haven: Yale University Press, 1912. 578pp.

The Self, its Body and Freedom. New Haven: Yale University Press, 1928. 178pp.

Thoughts on Life and Death. New York: Harper and Brothers, 1937. 255pp.

Types of Philosophy. New York: Charles Scribner's Sons, 1929. 462pp.

What Man Can Make of Man. New York: Harper and Brothers, 1942. 62pp.

Essays

"Mind and Near-Mind", *Proceedings of the Sixth International Congress of Philosophy*. Edgar S. Brightman, editor; New York: Longmans, Green, and Co., 1927. Pp. 471-499.

"Some Second Principles", *Contemporary American Philosophy*. G. P. Adams and W. P. Montague, editors; New York: The Macmillan Co., 1930. Two Vols.. Vol. I, pp. 383-400.

Periodical Articles

"Action and Certainty", *The Journal of Philosophy*. XXVII:9, April 24, 1930. Pp. 225-238.

"Dewey's Concepts of Experience and Nature", *The Philosophical Review*, XLIX:2, March, 1940. Pp. 335-342.

"Does Civilization Still Need Religion?", *Christendom*, I:1, October 1925. Pp. 31-45.

"Mysticism as Seen Through its Psychology", *Mind*, N.S., XXI:81, January, 1912. Pp. 38-62.

"The Illicit Naturalising of Religion", *The Journal of Religion*, III:6, November, 1923. Pp. 561-589.

MACINTOSH, DOUGLAS CLYDE

Books

God in a World at War. London: George Allen and Unwin, Ltd., 1918. 59pp.

Personal Religion. New York: Charles Scribner's Sons, 1942. 411pp.

Social Religion. New York: Charles Scribner's Sons, 1939. 336pp.

The Pilgrimage of Faith in the World of Modern Thought. Calcutta: University of Calcutta, 1931. 299pp.

The Problem of Knowledge. New York: The Macmillan Co., 1915. 503pp.

The Problem of Religious Knowledge. New York: Harper and Brothers, 1940. 390pp.

The Reasonableness of Christianity. New York: Charles Scribner's Sons, 1925. 293pp.

Theology as an Empirical Science. New York: The Macmillan Co., 1919 (Second edition, 1927). 270pp.

Essays

"Experimental Realism in Religion", *Religious Realism.* Douglas C. Macintosh, editor; New York: The Macmillan Co., 1931. Pp. 303-409.

Is There a God? Various essays, with M. C. Otto and H. N. Wieman; C. C. Morrison, editor; Chicago: Willet, Clark, and Co., 1932. 328pp.

The Reaction Against Metaphysics in Theology. Doctoral dissertation, published privately; Chicago: The University of Chicago, 1911, 86pp.

"Theology in a Scientific Age", *Education for Christian Service.* Faculty of the Divinity School of Yale University; New Haven: Yale University Press, 1922. Pp. 133-162.

"Toward a New Untraditional Orthodoxy", *Contemporary American Theology.* Vergilius Ferm, editor; New York: Round Table Press, 1932. Two Vols., Vol. I, Pp. 277-323.

"What God Is", *My Idea of God,* Joseph F. Newton, editor; Boston: Little, Brown, and Co., 1927. Pp. 137-158.

Periodical Articles

"Empirical Theology and Some of its Misunderstanders", *The Review of Religion,* III:4, May, 1939. Pp. 385-398.

"Hocking's Philosophy of Religion", *The Philosophical Review,* XXIII: January, 1914. Pp. 27-47.

"Is Belief in the Historicity of Jesus Indispensable to the Christian Faith?", *American Journal of Theology,* XV: July, 1911. Pp. 362-372.

"Mr. Wieman and Mr. Macintosh Converse with Mr. Dewey", *The Christian Century,* L: March 1, 1933. Pp. 300-302.

"Personal Idealism, Pragmatism, and the New Realism", *American Journal of Theology,* XIV: October, 1910. Pp. 650-656.

"Professor Coe and an Empirical Theology", *The Methodist Quarterly Review,* LXXVI: April, 1927. Pp. 202-218.

"Religious Knowledge and Religious Faith", *Colgate-Rochester Divinity School Bulletin,* II: November, 1929. Pp. 160-174.

"Religious Values and the Existence of God", *The Journal of Religion,* VI: May, 1926. Pp. 315-320.

"The Next Step in the Epistemological Dialectic", *The Journal of Philosophy,* XXVI: April, 1929. Pp. 225-233.

"The New Christianity and World Conversion", *American Journal of Theology,* XVIII: October, 1914. Pp. 553-570.

"The Religious Philosophy of W. E. Hocking", *Yale Divinity Quarterly*, X:3, January, 1914. Pp. 73-78.
"Theology, Valuational or Existential?" *The Review of Religion*, IV:1, November, 1939. Pp. 22-41.
"What Has Professor Brightman Done to Personalism?", *Religion in Life*, I: Spring, 1932. Pp. 304-307.

WIEMAN, HENRY NELSON
Books

American Philosophies of Religion. (With Bernard E. Meland) Chicago: Willett, Clark, and Co., 1936. 370pp.
Methods of Private Religious Living. New York: The Macmillan Co., 1929. Other editions 1931 and 1938. 219pp.
Normative Psychology of Religion. (With Regina W. Wieman) New York: Thomas Y. Crowell Co., 1935. 564pp.
Religious Experience and Scientific Method. New York: The Macmillan Co., 1927. 256pp.
The Growth of Religion. (With Walter M. Horton) Chicago: Willett, Clark, and Co., 1938. 505pp.
The Issues of Life. New York: The Abingdon Press, 1930. 273pp.
The Wrestle of Religion with Truth. New York: The Macmillan Co., 1927. 256pp.

Essays

Is There a God? Various essays with D. C. Macintosh and M. C. Otto; C. C. Morrison, editor; Chicago: Willett, Clark, and Co., 1932. 382pp.
"The Scientific Method and the Christian Gospel". Pamphlet. Madison, N. J.: Conference of Theological Seminaries, 1929. 7pp.
"Theocentric Religion", *Contemporary American Theology*, Vergilius Ferm, editor; New York: Round Table Press, 1932. Two Vols. Vol. I, pp. 339-351.
"God and Value", *Religious Realism*, D. C. Macintosh, editor; New York: The Macmillan Co., 1931. Pp. 155-179.

Periodical Articles

"Another Interpretation of St. Francis", *The Christian Century*, XLVII:7, Feb. 12, 1930. Pp. 206-211.
"Authority and the Normative Approach", *The Journal of Religion*, XVI:2, April, 1936. Pp. 184-202.
"Can God Be Perceived?" *The Journal of Religion*, XXIII:1, January 1943. Pp. 23-32.
Communication, *The Journal of Religion*, XXIV:1, January, 1944. Pp. 56-58.
"Experience, Mind, and the Concept", *The Journal of Philosophy*, XXI:21, Oct. 9, 1924. Pp. 561-567.

"Faith and Knowledge", *Christendom*, I:5, Autumn, 1936. Pp. 762-778.

"God is More Than We Can Think", *Christendom*, I:3, Spring, 1936. Pp. 428-442.

"God, the Inescapable", *The Christian Century*, XLVIII:38, 39, Sept. 23 and 30, 1931. Pp. 1170-1172, 1209-1221.

"How Do We Know?", *The Christian Century*, XLVIII:21, May 27, 1931. Pp. 711-715.

"How Do We Know God?", *The Journal of Religion*, V:2, March, 1925. Pp. 113-129.

"Perception and Cognition", *The Journal of Philosophy*, XL:3, Feb. 4, 1943. Pp. 73-77.

"Religion in John Dewey's Philosophy", *The Journal of Religion*, XI:1, January, 1931. Pp. 3-18.

"Religion in Dewey's Experience and Nature", *The Journal of Religion*, V:5, September, 1925. Pp. 519-542.

Review of Bewkes, *et al, The Nature of Religious Experience, Christendom*, II:3, Summer, 1937. Pp. 497-501.

Review of Edgar S. Brightman, *A Philosophy of Religion, The Journal of Religion*, XXL:2, April, 1941. Pp. 197-200.

Review of Ralph T. Flewelling, *Creative Personality, The Journal of Religion*, VII:7, pp. 321-323.

Review of Albert C. Knudson, *The Philosophy of Personalism, The Journal of Religion*, VIII:2, April, 1927. Pp. 291-296.

Review of Henry P. Van Dusen, *The Plain Man Seeks for God, The Journal of Religion*, XIV:1, January, 1934. Pp. 117-119.

"Right Ways to Justify Religion", *The Christian Century*, XLVII:5, Jan. 29, 1930. Pp. 139-142.

"Some Blind Spots Removed", *The Christian Century*, LVI:4, Jan. 25, 1939. Pp. 115-119.

"The Absolute Commitment of Faith", *Christendom*, II:2, Spring, 1937. Pp. 202-214.

"The Power and Goodness of God", *The Journal of Religion*, XXIII:4, October, 1943. Pp. 266-276.

"Theology and the Philosophy of Religion", *The Journal of Liberal Religion*, II:4, Spring, 1941. Pp. 163-175.

"Values and the Individual", *The Journal of Philosophy*, XXV:9, April 26, 1928. Pp. 233-239.

"Values: Primary Data for Religious Inquiry", *The Journal of Religion*, XVI:4, October, 1936. Pp. 379-405.

GENERAL

Books

Anderson, Paul R., and Max H. Fisch, editors; *Philosophy in America*. New York: D. Appleton-Century Co., 1939. 541pp.

Aubrey, Edwin E., *Present Theological Tendencies*. New York: Harper and Brothers, 1936. 245pp.

Ayer, Alfred J., *The Foundations of Empirical Knowledge*. New York: The Macmillan Co., 1940. 276pp.

Bertocci, Peter A., *The Empirical Argument for God in Late British Thought*. Cambridge: Harvard University Press, 1938. 311pp.

Bixler, Julius S., *Religion in the Philosophy of William James*. Boston: Marshall Jones Co., 1926. 225pp.

Burtt, Edwin A., *Types of Religious Philosophy*. New York: Harper and Brothers, 1939. 512pp.

Dewey, John, *A Common Faith*. New Haven: Yale University Press, 1934. 87pp.

———, *Experience and Nature*. New York: W. W. Norton Co., 1929. 437pp.

———, Logic: *The Theory of Inquiry*. New York: Henry Holt and Co., 1938. 546pp.

James, William, *Essays on Radical Empiricism*. New York: Longmans, Green, and Co., 1912. 279pp.

———, *Pragmatism*. New York: Longmans, Green, and Co., 1907. 301pp.

———, *The Will to Believe*. New York: Longmans, Green, and Co., 1911, 327pp.

———, *The Varieties of Religious Experience*. New York: Longmans, Green, and Co., 1902. 534pp.

Kroner, Richard, *How Do We Know God?* New York: Harper and Brothers, 1943. 132pp.

Lewis, Clarence I., *Mind and the World Order*. New York: Charles Scribner's Sons, 1929. 446pp.

Mackintosh, Hugh R., *Types of Modern Theology*. London: Nisbet and Co., Ltd., 1937. 333pp.

Mackintosh, Robert, *Albrecht Ritschl and His School*. London: Chapman and Hall, Ltd., 1915. 285pp.

Montague, William P., *The Ways of Knowing*. New York: The Macmillan Co., 1936. 427pp.

Moore, Edward C., *An Outline of the History of Christian Thought Since Kant*. New York: Charles Scribner's Sons, 1916. 249pp.

Moore, John M., *Theories of Religious Experience*. New York: Round Table Press, 1938. 253pp.

Muelder, Walter E., and Laurence Sears, editors; *The Development of American Philosophy*. New York: Houghton, Mifflin Co., 1940.

Ratner, Joseph, Editor; *Intelligence in the Modern World: John Dewey's Philosophy*. New York: The Modern Library, 1939. 1069pp.

Ritschl, Albrecht, *The Christian Doctrine of Justification and Reconciliation*. H. R. Mackintosh and A. B. Macauley, editors; Edinburgh: T. and T. Clark, 1900. 673pp.

Royce, Josiah, *The Problem of Christianity*. New York: The Macmillan Co., 1919. Two Vols.

———, *The Religious Aspects of Philosophy*. Boston: Houghton, Mifflin Co., 1887. 484pp.

———, *Sources of Religious Insight*. New York: Charles Scribner's Sons, 1923. 287pp.

———, *William James, and Other Essays*, New York: The Macmillan Co., 1911. 301pp.

Urban, Wilbur M., *Language and Realty*. London: George Allen and Unwin, Ltd., 1939. 755pp.

Wieman, Henry N., and Eugene B. Melan, *American Philosophies of Religion*. Chicago: Willett, Clark, and Co., 1936. 359pp.

Essays

Dewey, John, "An Empirical Survey of Empiricisms", *Studies in the Histories of Ideas*. Vol. III, New York: Columbia University Press, 1935. Pp. 3-22.

Lamprecht, Sterling P., "Empiricism and Natural Knowledge", *University of California Press*, 1940. Pp. 71-94.

Randall, John Herman, Jr., "The Religion of Shared Experience", *The Philosopher of the Common Man: Essays in Honor of John Dewey*. New York: G. P. Putnam's Sons, 1940. Pp. 106-146.

Religious Realism, D. C. Macintosh, editor; New York: The Macmillan Co., 1931. 502pp. Esp. H. Richard Niebuhr, "Religious Realism in the Twentieth Century, pp. 413-431; Alban G. Widgery, "Religious Realism and the Empirical Facts of Religion", Pp. 101-133.

Schneider, Herbert W., "Radical Empiricism in Religion", *Essays in Honor of John Dewey*. New York: Henry Holt and Co., 1929. Pp. 336-354.

The Nature of Religious Experience. J. S. Bixler, R. L. Calhoun, and H. R. Niebuhr, editors; New York: Harper and Brothers, 1937. 244pp. Esp. Eugene G. Bewkes, "Common Sense Realism", Pp. 1-26; Julius S. Bixler, "Can Religion Become Empirical"?, pp. 68-93; H. R. Niebuhr, "Value Theory and Theology", pp. 93-116; Reinhold Niebuhr, "The Truth in Myths", pp. 117-136.

Periodical Articles

Aubrey, Edwin E., "The Authority of Religious Experience Re-Examined", *The Journal of Religion*. XIII:4, October, 1933. Pp. 33-49.

Bernhardt, W. H., "The Cognitive Quest for God", *The Journal of Religion*. XXIII:2, April, 1943. Pp. 91-103.

Bertocci, Peter A., "Macintosh's Theory of Natural Knowledge", *The Journal of Religion*, XXIII:3, July, 1943. Pp. 164-172.

———, "An Analysis of Macintosh's Theory of Religious Knowledge", *The Journal of Religion*, XXIV:1, January, 1944. Pp. 42-45.

Bixler, Julius S., "The Spirit and the Life", *The Review of Religion*, I:2, January, 1937. Pp. 113-135.

Calhoun, Robert L., "God as More Than Mind", *Christendom*. I: II, Winter 1936. Pp. 333-349.

————, "How Shall We Think of God?", *Christendom*. I:4, Summer, 1936, pp. 593-611; "The Power of God and the Wisdom of God", II:1, Winter 1937, pp. 36-49; "A Final Statement", II:2, Spring, 1937, pp. 215-218.

De Burgh, W. G., Review of Edgar S. Brightman, *A Philosophy of Religion*. *Mind*. N.S., XLIX:196, October, 1940. Pp. 480-486.

Dewey, John, "Mr. Wieman and Mr. Macintosh Converse with Mr. Dewey", *The Christian Century*. L: March 1, 1933. Pp. 300-302.

Dubs, H. H., "Religious Naturalism—An Evaluation", *The Journal of Religion*. XXIII:4, October, 1943. Pp. 258-266.

Lamprecht, Sterling P., Review of P. A. Bertocci, *The Empirical Argument for God in Late British Thought*, *The Journal of Philosophy*. XXXVI:3, Feb. 2, 1939. Discussion, *ibid*. XXXVI:10, May 11, 1939. Pp. 263-274.

Leuba, James H., "The Immediate Apprehension of God According to William James and William E. Hocking", *The Journal of Philosophy*. XXI:26, Dec. 18, 1924. Pp. 701-712.

Loewenberg, J., "What is Empirical?", *The Journal of Philosophy*, XXXVII:11, May 23, 1940. Pp. 281-285.

Ohrenstein, Edward W., "Language and Liberal Religion", *The Journal of Liberal Religion*. II:1, Summer, 1940. Pp. 1-12.

Schneider, H. W., "Theology and Science in Contemporary Platonic Idealism", *The Review of Religion*. II:2, January, 1938. Pp. 166-174.

Tillich, Paul, "The Religious Symbol", *The Journal of Liberal Religion*, II:1, Summer, 1940. Pp. 13-33.

Walker, Edwin R., "Can Philosophy of Religion Be Empirical?", *The Journal of Religion*. XIX:4, October, 1939, pp. 315-330. Discussion by George F. Thomas, John C. Bennett, and David E. Roberts, XX:2, April, 1940, pp. 169-177.